Chinese Horoscope for 1994

About the Author

Neil Somerville is one of the leading writers in the West on Chinese horoscopes. He has been interested in Eastern forms of divination for many years and believes that much can be learned from the ancient wisdom of the East. His annual book on Chinese horoscopes has built up an international following and *Your Chinese Horoscope for 1994* marks the seventh year of publication.

Neil Somerville was born in the year of the Water Snake. His wife was born under the sign of the Monkey, his son is an Ox and daughter a Horse.

Your Chinese Horoscope for 1994

Neil Somerville

What the Year of the Dog holds in store for you

Aquarian/Thorsons
An Imprint of HarperCollins*Publishers*

The Aquarian Press
An Imprint of HarperCollins*Publishers*
77–85 Fulham Palace Road,
Hammersmith, London W6 8JB

Published by The Aquarian Press 1993
1 3 5 7 9 10 8 6 4 2

© Neil Somerville 1993

Neil Somerville asserts the moral right to
be identified as the author of this work.

Illustrations by John Davis

A catalogue record for this book
is available from the British Library

ISBN 1 85538 290 3

Typeset by Harper Phototypesetters Limited,
Northampton, England
Printed in Great Britain by
HarperCollinsManufacturing Glasgow

All rights reserved. No part of this publication may be
reproduced, stored in a retrieval system, or transmitted,
in any form or by any means, electronic, mechanical,
photocopying, recording or otherwise, without the prior
permission of the publishers.

Contents

Introduction 7
The Chinese Years 9
Welcome to the Year of the Dog 13

The Rat 19
The Ox 33
The Tiger 47
The Rabbit 61
The Dragon 75
The Snake 91
The Horse 105
The Goat 119
The Monkey 133
The Rooster 149
The Dog 163
The Pig 177

Appendix: Relationships 192
Your Ascendant 194
How to Get the Best from the Year 196

To Ros, Richard and Emily.

Introduction

The origins of Chinese horoscopes have been lost in the mists of time. It is known that oriental astrologers practised their art many thousands of years ago and, even today, Chinese astrology continues to fascinate and intrigue.

In Chinese astrology there are 12 signs named after 12 different animals. No one quite knows how the signs acquired their names, but there is one legend that offers an explanation.

According to this legend, one Chinese New Year, the Buddha invited all the animals in his kingdom to come before him. Unfortunately – for reasons best known to the animals – only 12 turned up. The first to arrive was the Rat, followed by the Ox, Tiger, Rabbit, Dragon, Snake, Horse, Goat, Monkey, Rooster, Dog and finally the Pig.

In gratitude, the Buddha decided to name a year after each of the animals and those born during that year would inherit some of the personality of that animal. Therefore those born in the year of the Ox would be hard working, resolute and stubborn – just like the Ox – while those born in the year of the Dog would be loyal and faithful – just like the Dog.

While not everyone can possibly share all the characteristics of a sign, it is incredible what similarities do occur, and this is partly where the fascination of Chinese horoscopes lies.

In addition to the 12 signs of the Chinese zodiac there are also 5 elements and these have a strengthening or moderating influence upon the sign. Details about the effects of the elements are given in each of the chapters on the 12 signs.

To find out which sign you were born under, refer to the tables on pages 9–11. As the Chinese year is based on the lunar year and does not start until late January or early February, it is particularly important for anyone born in those two months to check carefully the dates of the Chinese year in which they were born.

Also included, in the Appendix, are two charts showing the compatibility between the signs for both personal and business relationships, and details about the signs ruling the different hours of the day. From this it is possible to locate your ascendant and, as in Western astrology, this has a significant influence on your personality.

In writing this book, I have taken the unusual step of combining the intriguing nature of Chinese horoscopes with the Western desire to know what the future holds, and have based my interpretations upon various factors relating to each of the signs. This is the seventh year in which *Your Chinese Horoscope* has been published and I am pleased that so many have found the sections on the forthcoming year of benefit and that the advice has been constructive and helpful. Remember, though, that at all times you are the master of your own destiny. I sincerely hope that your Chinese horoscope for 1994 will prove interesting and helpful for the year ahead.

The Chinese Years

Rat	31 January 1900	to	18 February 1901
Ox	19 February 1901	to	7 February 1902
Tiger	8 February 1902	to	28 January 1903
Rabbit	29 January 1903	to	15 February 1904
Dragon	16 February 1904	to	3 February 1905
Snake	4 February 1905	to	24 January 1906
Horse	25 January 1906	to	12 February 1907
Goat	13 February 1907	to	1 February 1908
Monkey	2 February 1908	to	21 January 1909
Rooster	22 January 1909	to	9 February 1910
Dog	10 February 1910	to	29 January 1911
Pig	30 January 1911	to	17 February 1912
Rat	18 February 1912	to	5 February 1913
Ox	6 February 1913	to	25 January 1914
Tiger	26 January 1914	to	13 February 1915
Rabbit	14 February 1915	to	2 February 1916
Dragon	3 February 1916	to	22 January 1917
Snake	23 January 1917	to	10 February 1918
Horse	11 February 1918	to	31 January 1919
Goat	1 February 1919	to	19 February 1920
Monkey	20 February 1920	to	7 February 1921
Rooster	8 February 1921	to	27 January 1922
Dog	28 January 1922	to	15 February 1923
Pig	16 February 1923	to	4 February 1924
Rat	5 February 1924	to	24 January 1925
Ox	25 January 1925	to	12 February 1926
Tiger	13 February 1926	to	1 February 1927
Rabbit	2 February 1927	to	22 January 1928
Dragon	23 January 1928	to	9 February 1929

Snake	10 February 1929	to	29 January 1930
Horse	30 January 1930	to	16 February 1931
Goat	17 February 1931	to	5 February 1932
Monkey	6 February 1932	to	25 January 1933
Rooster	26 January 1933	to	13 February 1934
Dog	14 February 1934	to	3 February 1935
Pig	4 February 1935	to	23 January 1936
Rat	24 January 1936	to	10 February 1937
Ox	11 February 1937	to	30 January 1938
Tiger	31 January 1938	to	18 February 1939
Rabbit	19 February 1939	to	7 February 1940
Dragon	8 February 1940	to	26 January 1941
Snake	27 January 1941	to	14 February 1942
Horse	15 February 1942	to	4 February 1943
Goat	5 February 1943	to	24 January 1944
Monkey	25 January 1944	to	12 February 1945
Rooster	13 February 1945	to	1 February 1946
Dog	2 February 1946	to	21 January 1947
Pig	22 January 1947	to	9 February 1948
Rat	10 February 1948	to	28 January 1949
Ox	29 January 1949	to	16 February 1950
Tiger	17 February 1950	to	5 February 1951
Rabbit	6 February 1951	to	26 January 1952
Dragon	27 January 1952	to	13 February 1953
Snake	14 February 1953	to	2 February 1954
Horse	3 February 1954	to	23 January 1955
Goat	24 January 1955	to	11 February 1956
Monkey	12 February 1956	to	30 January 1957
Rooster	31 January 1957	to	17 February 1958
Dog	18 February 1958	to	7 February 1959
Pig	8 February 1959	to	27 January 1960
Rat	28 January 1960	to	14 February 1961
Ox	15 February 1961	to	4 February 1962
Tiger	5 February 1962	to	24 January 1963
Rabbit	25 January 1963	to	12 February 1964
Dragon	13 February 1964	to	1 February 1965
Snake	2 February 1965	to	20 January 1966

Horse	21 January 1966	to	8 February 1967
Goat	9 February 1967	to	29 January 1968
Monkey	30 January 1968	to	16 February 1969
Rooster	17 February 1969	to	5 February 1970
Dog	6 February 1970	to	26 January 1971
Pig	27 January 1971	to	14 February 1972
Rat	15 February 1972	to	2 February 1973
Ox	3 February 1973	to	22 January 1974
Tiger	23 January 1974	to	10 February 1975
Rabbit	11 February 1975	to	30 January 1976
Dragon	31 January 1976	to	17 February 1977
Snake	18 February 1977	to	6 February 1978
Horse	7 February 1978	to	27 January 1979
Goat	28 January 1979	to	15 February 1980
Monkey	16 February 1980	to	4 February 1981
Rooster	5 February 1981	to	24 January 1982
Dog	25 January 1982	to	12 February 1983
Pig	13 February 1983	to	1 February 1984
Rat	2 February 1984	to	19 February 1985
Ox	20 February 1985	to	8 February 1986
Tiger	9 February 1986	to	28 January 1987
Rabbit	29 January 1987	to	16 February 1988
Dragon	17 February 1988	to	5 February 1989
Snake	6 February 1989	to	26 January 1990
Horse	27 January 1990	to	14 February 1991
Goat	15 February 1991	to	3 February 1992
Monkey	4 February 1992	to	22 January 1993
Rooster	23 January 1993	to	9 February 1994
Dog	10 February 1994	to	30 January 1995

Note: The names of the signs in the Chinese zodiac occasionally differ in the various books on Chinese astrology, although the characteristics of the signs remain the same. In some books the Ox is referred to as the Buffalo or Bull, the Rabbit as the Hare or Cat, the Goat as the Sheep and the Pig as the Boar.

For the sake of convenience, the male gender is used throughout this book. Unless otherwise stated, the characteristics of the signs apply to both sexes.

Luck has a habit of visiting the industrious, the vigilant and the brave.

Oriental proverb.

Welcome to the Year of the Dog

It has often been said that a dog is a man's best friend. Whether as a loyal and loving pet, or as a guide dog, guard dog, sheep dog or mountain rescuer, the dog does provide an important service to mankind. And this sense of duty, of care and loyalty, so much a feature of the dog, will be much in evidence in 1994.

The Year of the Dog begins on 10 February 1994 and over the course of the year there will be an increasing emphasis on the role of society towards the individual. Many governments around the world will introduce measures to assist the less fortunate, to reduce the level of unemployment and to improve safety and the general way of life. In Britain, for instance, Dog years have seen the introduction of Labour Exchanges to help the unemployed, Litter Acts, Clean Air Acts and, to improve the safety of motorists and their passengers, the compulsory wearing of seat belts. Further significant measures will be introduced in 1994 and this sense of care and responsibility towards the individual will be much in evidence throughout the year.

It is also likely that several international conferences will be held so that concerted efforts can be made to tackle some of the problems of the current age. Environmental matters will have considerable prominence and issues such as pollution, the disposal of toxic waste, the destruction of the rain forests and the depletion of the ozone layer will receive much attention. The world's first Earth Day was held in the Year of the Dog and in 1994 positive steps will be taken to deal with environmental problems.

Humanitarian matters also feature prominently in Dog years and particular attention will be given to ways to help those countries that have been badly affected by famine and drought in recent years. New farming methods will be encouraged and attempts will be made to prevent the reoccurrence of these tragedies.

The Year of the Dog also tends to inspire a sense of patriotism and there will be increased support for nationalist causes. This could, however, cause problems for several world leaders, particularly those actively seeking closer international alignment. It should also be mentioned that this rise in nationalist fervour has in the past had unfortunate results. It was, for instance, a Dog year when the Argentineans invaded the Falkland Islands, territory they had long considered their own, and previous Dog years have seen other acts inspired by national pride which have resulted in armed conflict. Similarly, any acts of armed aggression that do take place over the year will be met by strong resistance, both military and political. The Dog is a great defender of property!

Interest groups will also be active in bringing their causes to the attention of governments. It was a Dog year when Lord Russell launched the Campaign for Nuclear Disarmament and the first CND march from London to Aldermaston took place. In the last Year of the Dog, 1982, hundreds of thousands demonstrated in New York's Central Park against nuclear arms and that same year 30,000 women formed a human chain around the Greenham Common missile base in the UK. In 1994 there will almost certainly be major rallies and protests, and quite often these will have a significant bearing on future government policy.

Politically, Dog years have generally favoured the Left and it is likely that several countries will see socialists and liberal-thinking politicians winning increased support for their views. A number of countries will also see significant changes in their constitutions over the year. It was the Year of the Dog when Portugal and Italy became republics, when the fifth French Republic was formed, when Egypt became independent and when the Union of Soviet Socialist Republics was established.

This pattern of constitutional change is likely to continue in 1994, involving particularly countries in Eastern Europe and the Middle East. Several countries will also see important changes in their leadership over the year and some of those who do come to power in Dog years often go on to play an important and historic role in world affairs. General de Gaulle, Dr Helmut Kohl and Nikita Khrushchev are just three leaders who were appointed to high office during the Year of the Dog.

As far as economic matters are concerned, the year will see a gradual improvement in many of the economies around the world. The building and property market in particular, which has been depressed for several years, will see a noticeable upturn. However, while economic trends will be a little more encouraging, there is still a need for investors to exercise a certain amount of caution. Previous Dog years have seen the collapse of major companies, including Laker Airways and the De Lorean car company, and 1994 is unlikely to be an exception.

On a more positive note, the Year of the Dog can be a particularly fulfilling year for the individual. It is a good time to undertake further study and to expand on skills and experience. It is also a good year for domestic and joint activities, particularly around the home, and many couples and families will obtain much satisfaction from projects that they carry out together. The Year of the Dog is also considered a most favourable year to get married!

This will undoubtedly be an interesting year and, for many, a satisfying and enjoyable one. In the chapters that follow you can discover how you and those close to you will fare. Naturally not all signs will fare as well as others, but in general the Year of the Dog is a positive one and by setting about activities diligently, pursuing opportunities and using spare time wisely, almost all will benefit from the Dog's caring influence. I sincerely hope that 1994 will be a good, healthy and prosperous year for you.

The Rat

31 January 1900 to	18 February 1901	*Metal Rat*
18 February 1912 to	5 February 1913	*Water Rat*
5 February 1924 to	24 January 1925	*Wood Rat*
24 January 1936 to	10 February 1937	*Fire Rat*
10 February 1948 to	28 January 1949	*Earth Rat*
28 January 1960 to	14 February 1961	*Metal Rat*
15 February 1972 to	2 February 1973	*Water Rat*
2 February 1984 to	19 February 1985	*Wood Rat*

The Personality of the Rat

> One man in his time plays many parts.
> – *William Shakespeare: a Rat.*

The Rat is born under the sign of charm. He is intelligent, popular, and loves attending parties and large social gatherings. He is able to establish friendships with remarkable ease and people generally feel relaxed in his company. He is a very social creature and is genuinely interested in the welfare and activities of others. He has a good understanding of human nature and his advice and opinions are often sought.

The Rat is a hard and diligent worker. He is also very imaginative and is never short of ideas. However, he does sometimes lack the confidence to promote his ideas as much as he should and this can often prevent him from securing the recognition and credit he so often deserves.

The Rat is very observant and there are many who have made excellent writers and journalists. He also excels at personnel and PR work and any job which brings him into contact with people and the media. His skills are particularly appreciated in times of crisis, for the Rat has an incredibly strong sense of self-preservation. When it comes to finding a way out of an awkward situation, he is certain to be the one who comes up with a solution.

The Rat loves to be where there is a lot of action, but should he ever find himself in a very bureaucratic or restrictive environment he can become a stickler for discipline and routine.

He is also something of an opportunist and is constantly on the look-out for ways in which he can improve his wealth and lifestyle. He rarely lets an opportunity go by and can become involved in so many plans and schemes that he sometimes squanders his energies and achieves very little as a result. He is also rather gullible and can be taken in by those less scrupulous than himself.

Another characteristic of the Rat is his attitude to money. He is very thrifty and to some he may appear a little mean. The reason for this is purely that he likes to keep his money within his family. He can be most generous to his partner, his children, and close friends and relatives. He can also be generous to himself, for he often finds it impossible to deprive himself of any luxury or object which he fancies. The Rat is also very acquisitive and can be a notorious hoarder. He hates waste and is rarely prepared to throw anything away. He can also be rather greedy and will rarely refuse an invitation for a free meal or a complimentary ticket to some lavish function.

The Rat is a good conversationalist, although he can occasionally be a little indiscreet. He can be highly critical of others – for an honest and unbiased opinion, the Rat is a superb critic – and sometimes will use confidential information to his own advantage. However, as the Rat has such a bright and irresistible nature, most are prepared to forgive him for his slight indiscretions.

Throughout his long and eventful life, the Rat will make many friends and will find that he is especially well-suited to those born under his own sign and those of the Ox, Dragon and Monkey. The Rat can also get on well with those born under the signs of the Tiger, Snake, Rooster, Dog and Pig, but the rather sensitive Rabbit and Goat will find the Rat a little too critical and blunt for their liking. The Horse and Rat will also find it difficult to get on with each other – the Rat craves security and will find the Horse's changeable moods and rather independent nature a little unsettling.

The Rat is very family orientated and will do anything to please his nearest and dearest. He is exceptionally loyal to his parents and can himself be a very caring and loving parent. He will take an interest in all his children's activities and will see that they want for nothing. The Rat usually has a large family.

The female Rat has a kindly, outgoing nature and involves herself in a multitude of different activities. She is a superb hostess and will usually have a wide circle of very good friends. She is conscientious about the upkeep of her home and has superb taste in home furnishings. She is extremely supportive to the other members of her family and, due to her resourceful, friendly and persevering nature, can do well in practically any career she enters.

Although the Rat is essentially outgoing and something of an extrovert, he is also a very private individual. He tends to keep his feelings to himself and, while he is not averse to learning what other people are doing, he resents anyone prying too closely into his own affairs. The Rat also does not like solitude and if he is alone for any length of time he can easily get depressed.

The Rat is undoubtedly very talented but more often than not he fails to capitalize on his many abilities. He has a tendency to become involved in too many schemes and chase after too many opportunities all at one time. If he were to slow down and concentrate on one thing at a time he could become very successful. If not, success and wealth could elude him. But the Rat, with his tremendous ability to charm, will rarely, if ever, be without friends.

The Five Different Types of Rat

In addition to the 12 signs of the Chinese zodiac, there are five elements and these have a strengthening or moderating influence on the sign. The effects of the five elements on the Rat are described below, together with the years in which the elements were exercising their influence. Therefore all Rats born in 1900 and 1960 are Metal Rats, those born in 1912 and 1972 are Water Rats, and so on.

Metal Rat: 1900, 1960
This Rat has excellent taste and certainly knows how to appreciate the finer things in life. His home is comfortable and nicely decorated and he is forever entertaining or mixing in fashionable circles. He has considerable financial acumen and invests his money well. On the surface the Metal Rat appears cheerful and confident, but deep down he can be troubled by worries that are quite often of his own making. He is exceptionally loyal to his family and friends.

Water Rat: 1912, 1972
The Water Rat is intelligent and very astute. He is a deep thinker and can express his thoughts clearly and persuasively. He is always eager to learn and is talented in many different areas. The Water Rat is usually very popular but his fear of loneliness can sometimes lead him into mixing with the wrong sort of company. He is a particularly skilful writer, but he can get side-tracked very easily and should try to concentrate on just one thing at a time.

Wood Rat: 1924, 1984
The Wood Rat has a friendly, outgoing personality and is most popular with his colleagues and friends. He has a quick, agile brain and likes to turn his hand to anything he thinks may be useful. His one fear is insecurity, but given his intelligence and capabilities this fear is usually unfounded. He has a good sense of humour, enjoys travel and, due to his highly imaginative nature, can be a gifted writer or artist.

Fire Rat: 1936
The Fire Rat is rarely still and seems to have a never-ending supply of energy and enthusiasm. He loves being involved in the action – be it travel, following up new ideas, or campaigning for a cause in which he fervently believes. He is an original thinker and hates being bound by petty restrictions or the dictates of others. He can be forthright in his views, but can sometimes get carried away in the excitement of the moment and commit himself to various undertakings without checking what all the implications might be. He has a resilient nature and, with the right support, can often go far in life.

Earth Rat: 1948
This Rat is astute and very level-headed. He rarely takes unnecessary chances and, while he is constantly trying to improve his financial status, he is prepared to proceed slowly and leave nothing to chance. The Earth Rat is probably not as adventurous as the other types of Rat and prefers to remain in areas he knows rather than rush headlong into something he knows little about. He is talented, conscientious, and caring towards his loved ones, but at the same time can be self-conscious and worry a little too much about the image he is trying to project.

Prospects for the Rat in 1994

The Chinese New Year starts on 10 February 1994. Until then, the old year, the Year of the Rooster, is still making its presence felt.

The Year of the Rooster (23 January 1993 to 9 February 1994) will have been a busy but generally rewarding year for the Rat. Throughout the year he will have experienced many demands on his time and could also have seen some significant changes in his lifestyle. These could have involved a move, a change in his work or in his personal situation, and while these may have been unsettling or stressful, the end result could be to his long-term advantage. Indeed the Year of the Rooster is considered a significant year for the Rat and the positive results of his hard labours are likely to be seen in the closing stages of the year.

In what remains of the Year of the Rooster, the Rat should continue to set about his activities in a purposeful and determined manner. He can accomplish much at this time, finish outstanding matters and resolve any difficulties that he might have had. December 1993 and January 1994 can be two positive and rewarding months for the Rat.

The Rat is also likely to be much in demand with his family and friends over the Christmas and New Year holidays, and he will find the holiday period both enjoyable and a good time to unwind from the pressures of the year. He would also do well to give some thought to what he has accomplished over the last 12 months and to how he can build on his accomplishments. It would be a good time for him to consider his future objectives and set himself some goals to aim for. Very soon the Rat will be entering a new and positive phase of his life, and without some idea of the direction he would like to go, he could miss out on the very special opportunities that will be available to him in the new Chinese year.

The Year of the Dog starts on 10 February 1994 and will be a pleasing and constructive year for the Rat. Admittedly he will find progress in some areas of life easier than in others, but provided he sets about his activities in his usual persistent and good-natured manner, he will be able to end the year with some splendid gains to his credit.

One of the most favourably aspected areas for the Rat is work and business. He will find that he will be able to make considerable progress and that those around him will be supportive and co-operative. He should advance any new ideas that he has and, if he is involved in any creative undertaking, he is likely to find that this will be favourably received. Rats have many capabilities and are adept at identifying opportunities. In 1994 the Rat should put these talents to good use. By remaining alert he will spot some ideal opportunities which he can use to his advantage and, with determination and the right attitude, this can be an excellent year for advancing his career.

For those Rats seeking employment, there will also be several opportunities over the year to put talents and skills to good use. By remaining persistent, many Rats seeking work will be able to gain new and potentially rewarding positions, particularly in the first half of the year.

However, while work and business activities are favourably aspected, the Rat does need to exercise care where his personal finances are concerned. The Rat can sometimes be over-indulgent and throughout the year he would do well to watch his level of outgoings and avoid committing himself to any risky undertakings. This is just not a time when the Rat can afford to be either complacent or extravagant in money matters. If he is, he could experience financial problems later in the year – problems which, with care, could have been avoided.

There will also be occasions when the Rat will find that there are many demands on his time and that he will be under considerable pressure. When such a situation arises, he would do well to decide upon his priorities and to deal with existing affairs before starting any new undertaking. Sometimes, through over-enthusiasm and his willing nature, the Rat can involve himself in too many activities at the same time and this is something he would do well to avoid. He will also enjoy greater success if he concentrates on areas which are familiar to him rather than attempting anything too diverse or new.

The Rat will lead an active social life over the year, although he does still need to handle his relations with others with care. Sometimes he can be guilty of taking the support of others for granted and this is something he would do well to watch. He should try to involve those around him in his activities and be more open in expressing his views and opinions. Without care, misunderstandings could easily arise, which, with a little forethought, could have been avoided.

For any Rat who may have been lonely in recent times there will, however, be some excellent opportunities to make new friends and Rats should make every effort to go out more or perhaps join a local society which would bring them into contact with others. There will also be opportunities for romance over the year, but the unattached Rat would do well to let any new friendship develop in its own time rather than rush into any commitment. Romantic matters and relationships with others do need careful handling, but providing the Rat bears this in mind, he can look forward to some enjoyable and happy times and also to building up some good and worthwhile friendships.

While 1994 will be a generally positive year for the Rat, there will be a few problems that he will have to face. These are unlikely to be serious but, when dealing with any difficulty, the Rat would do well to seek the advice of those around him rather than try to solve the problem all by himself. He should also try to deal with any problem when it arises rather than to leave it to drag on or pretend it is not there. Quick and decisive action will often be in his best interests.

There will be several opportunities for the Rat to travel

over the year and he will find short breaks or holidays particularly beneficial. However, before undertaking any lengthy journey, it would be in his interests to ensure that all his travel documents are in order and that he is aware of any connections that he has to make. Without proper planning, his journeys could be prone to delays and disruptions and this could spoil what would otherwise be a good time away.

Generally, 1994 will be a favourable year for the Rat and he will enjoy his greatest successes in work matters. Here he should pursue any opportunities that he sees and make every effort to improve his present position. In this respect 1994 can be a most rewarding year for him. Most Rats will be given new responsibilities over the year or be successful in obtaining a new and more rewarding position. However, on a cautionary note, the Rat does need to handle his relations with others with care and also keep a careful check on that rather indulgent nature of his. If he bears this in mind, this can be a positive, constructive and generally enjoyable year for him.

As far as the different types of Rat are concerned, 1994 will prove an interesting and varied year for the **Metal Rat**. He will do well in most of his activities and will easily impress others with his friendly and determined manner. The Metal Rat will make good progress in his work over the year and would do well to advance any new ideas that he has and pursue any opportunities that he sees. In 1994 he can go a long way towards securing his goals and ambitions, but much does depend on his determination and also on his having a clear idea of his objectives. Without this, the Metal Rat could all too easily drift through parts of the year and not make the best use of his considerable capabilities and potential. The Metal Rat will also be quite busy throughout 1994, but he should not let the demands of his work and interests encroach too much on the time he spends with his loved ones. If he does, relationships which he values may become strained. The Metal Rat would also do well to keep a watch on his level of spending over the year. Sometimes he can be rather too generous or extravagant for his own good and it is a trait that he does need to watch. However, with sensible planning and clear goals, this can be a positive and fulfilling year for the Metal Rat. He will make progress in many of his activities and the year will hold many happy and enjoyable moments for him.

This will be an important year for the **Water Rat** and several significant changes will take place. These could involve either a new job, new accommodation or a change in his personal situation, but generally they will open up new opportunities for him and enable him to improve upon his present situation. Throughout the year the Water Rat needs to adopt and maintain a positive outlook and pursue any new openings that he sees. Provided he is persistent and determined, particularly where his work is concerned, 1994 can be a most rewarding and beneficial year for him. The Water Rat will also have some memorable times with his family and friends and many Water Rats will have good cause for a personal celebration during the year. However, despite his usually considerate nature, the Water Rat does still need to exercise care in his dealings with others and to avoid taking their support and backing for granted. If he has any worries, he should seek the views of others. The Water Rat also needs to exercise care in financial matters and if he is in doubt about the terms of any transaction he is about to enter, he should check all the clauses and implications of the agreement very carefully. In 1994, the Water Rat cannot afford to take risks or be too extravagant in his spending.

This will be a significant and important year for the **Wood Rat**. Although he may have to contend with a few small problems, they are unlikely to be serious and he will still be able to accomplish much over the year. He should set about his activities in his usual conscientious manner, and if there is anything that might be troubling him, no matter how small, the Wood Rat should not hesitate to seek the advice of those around him. He will be gratified by the support and encouragement he is given and also by the esteem and affection demonstrated. The year will also hold many happy and memorable moments for him and he is likely to obtain considerable pleasure from a new interest that he takes up, particularly if it is an outdoor activity or enables him to use his creative skills in any way. Many Wood Rats will move or have alterations carried out on their property and will be pleased with how this goes. However, on a cautionary note, the Wood Rat would be wise not to undertake any particularly strenuous or hazardous activity without the proper preparations or precautions. A strain or minor accident could cause him unnecessary suffering. Socially this will be quite an active year and most Wood Rats will find that their circle of friends and acquaintances will increase. The Wood Rat is also likely to attend some pleasant and memorable social functions in 1994 and any short breaks or holidays that he takes will prove enjoyable and beneficial for him.

This will be a reasonably good year for the **Fire Rat** and, providing he conducts his activities in a determined and responsible manner, he will be very satisfied with his progress. If, however, he acts in an impulsive manner – as he can sometimes be tempted to do – he could find the results that he seeks elusive and his relations with others becoming strained. In 1994 he should remember to act carefully, determinedly and diplomatically. If he does, this can be a most rewarding year for him. His work and business interests are most favourably aspected and many Fire Rats can look forward to obtaining a new position or to being given new responsibilities over the year. The Fire Rat should remain particularly alert for new opportunities to pursue in the early months of the year. Although he can look forward to an active and generally enjoyable social life, he does need to be careful in domestic matters. He should make every effort to set time aside to be with his family and loved ones. If not, and if he becomes too preoccupied with his own concerns, he could find tensions arising and his domestic life not being as smooth as he would like. Providing he heeds this warning, the year will hold many happy and satisfying moments for him.

This will be a busy but generally pleasing year for the **Earth Rat**. He will find that some of his plans and hopes for the year may be subject to delay or revision, but, provided he is prepared to be patient and adaptable, many of the events of the year will move in his favour. Indeed, the year favours persistent effort and the Earth Rat would do well to concentrate on specific areas rather than get involved in too many different activities all at the same time. He also needs to make sure that he has the support and co-operation of others before undertaking any major commitment – 1994 is, for the Earth Rat, a year for joint rather than independent action. The Earth Rat may also have a few problems to overcome during the year and while not serious, they could cause him worry. In some cases, he might feel that others are interfering unnecessarily in matters that do not really concern them. However, the Earth Rat would do well to listen carefully to all the advice he is given and some information from a close friend will prove especially helpful. The Earth Rat will obtain much satisfaction and pleasure from his family and social life over the year and he is likely to take particular pride in the achievements of a younger relation. If he feels able to offer any additional support or advice to this relation, this will be greatly appreciated and will do much good. The Earth Rat will notice a general upturn in his fortunes from the middle of 1994 onwards and July and September are likely to prove two important and significant months for him.

Famous Rats

Alan Alda, Dave Allen, Ursula Andress, Louis Armstrong, Charles Aznavour, Shirley Bassey, Irving Berlin, Virginia

Bottomley, Marlon Brando, Charlotte Brontë, Chris de Burgh, George Bush, Lord Callaghan, Jimmy Carter, Pablo Casals, Dick Cavett, Raymond Chandler, Maurice Chevalier, Linford Christie, Steve Cram, Barbara Dickson, Benjamin Disraeli, Elizabeth Dole, Noel Edmonds, T.S. Eliot, Ben Elton, Albert Finney, Sir Clement Freud, Clark Gable, Al Gore, Thomas Hardy, Vaclav Havel, Haydn, Charlton Heston, Benny Hill, Roy Hudd, Jeremy Irons, Glenda Jackson, Jean-Michel Jarre, Gene Kelly, F.W. de Klerk, Nastassja Kinski, Lawrence of Arabia, Ivan Lendl, Gary Lineker, Andrew Lloyd Webber, Lulu, Henri Mancini, Earl Mountbatten, Robert Mugabe, Olivia Newton-John, Richard Nixon, Robert Palmer, Sean Penn, Captain Mark Phillips, Enoch Powell, Prince, the Queen Mother, Vanessa Redgrave, Burt Reynolds, Jonathan Ross, Emma Samms, Ayrton Senna, William Shakespeare, Wayne Sleep, Yves St Laurent, Tommy Steele, Shakin' Stevens, Donna Summer, James Taylor, Leo Tolstoy, the Prince of Wales, Dennis Waterman, Roger Whittaker, Kim Wilde, the Duke of York.

The Ox

19 February 1901 to	7 February 1902	*Metal Ox*
6 February 1913 to	25 January 1914	*Water Ox*
25 January 1925 to	12 February 1926	*Wood Ox*
11 February 1937 to	30 January 1938	*Fire Ox*
29 January 1949 to	16 February 1950	*Earth Ox*
15 February 1961 to	4 February 1962	*Metal Ox*
3 February 1973 to	22 January 1974	*Water Ox*
20 February 1985 to	8 February 1986	*Wood Ox*

The Personality of the Ox

The truest wisdom is a resolute determination.
– *Napoleon Bonaparte: an Ox.*

The Ox is born under the signs of equilibrium and tenacity. He is a hard and conscientious worker and sets about everything he does in a resolute, methodical and determined manner. He has considerable leadership qualities and is often admired for his tough and uncompromising nature. He knows what he wants to achieve in life and, as far as possible, will not be deflected from his ultimate objective.

The Ox takes his responsibilities and duties very seriously. He is decisive and quick to take advantage of any opportunity that comes his way. He is also sincere and places a great deal of trust in his friends and colleagues. He is, nevertheless, something of a loner. He is a quiet and private individual and often keeps his thoughts to himself. He also cherishes his independence and prefers to set about things in his own way rather than be bound by the dictates of others or be influenced by outside pressures.

The Ox tends to have a calm and tranquil nature, but if something angers him or he feels that someone has let him down, he can have a fearsome temper. He can also be stubborn and obstinate and this can lead the Ox into conflict with others. Usually the Ox will succeed in getting his own way, but should things go against him, he is a poor loser and will take any defeat or set-back extremely badly.

The Ox is often a deep thinker and rather studious. He is not particularly renowned for his sense of humour and does not take kindly to new gimmicks or anything too innovative. The Ox is too solid and traditional for that and he prefers to stick to the more conventional norm.

His home is very important to him and in some respects he treats it as a private sanctuary. His family tends to be closely knit and the Ox will make sure that each member does their fair share around the house. The Ox tends to be a hoarder, but he is always well-organized and neat. He also places great importance on punctuality and there is nothing that infuriates him more than to be kept waiting – particularly if it is due to someone's inefficiency. The Ox can be a hard taskmaster!

Once settled in a job or house the Ox will quite happily remain there for many years. He does not like change and he is also not particularly keen on travel. He does, however, enjoy gardening and other outdoor pursuits and he will often spend much of his spare time out of doors. The Ox is usually an excellent gardener and whenever possible he will always make sure he has a large area of ground to maintain. The Ox usually prefers to live in the country rather than the town.

Due to his dedicated and dependable nature, he will usually do well in his chosen career, providing he is given enough freedom to act on his own initiative. He invariably does well in politics, agriculture, and in careers which need specialized training. The Ox is also very gifted in the arts and there are many who have enjoyed considerable success as musicians or composers.

The Ox is not as outgoing as some and it often takes him a long time to establish friendships and feel relaxed in another person's company. His courtships are likely to be long, but once he is settled he will remain devoted and loyal to his partner. The Ox is particularly well-suited to those born under the signs of the Rat, Rabbit, Snake and Rooster. He can also establish a good relationship with the Monkey, Dog, Pig and another Ox, but he will find that he has little in common with the whimsical and sensitive Goat. He will also find it difficult to get on with the Horse, Dragon and Tiger – the Ox prefers a quiet and peaceful existence and those born under these three signs tend to be a little too lively and impulsive for his liking.

The lady Ox has a kind and caring nature, and her home and family are very much her pride and joy. She always tries to do her best for her partner and can be a most conscientious and loving parent. The lady Ox is an excellent organizer and she is also a very determined person who will often succeed in getting what she wants in life. She usually has a deep interest in the arts and is often a talented artist or musician.

The Ox is a very down-to-earth character. He is sincere, loyal and unpretentious. He can, however, be rather reserved and to some he may appear distant and aloof. He has a quiet nature, but underneath he is very strong-willed and ambitious. He has the courage of his convictions and is often prepared to stand up for what he believes is right, regardless of the consequences. He inspires confidence and trust and throughout his life he will rarely be short of people who are ready to support him or who admire his strong and resolute manner.

The Five Different Types of Ox

In addition to the 12 signs of the Chinese zodiac, there are five elements and these have a strengthening or moderating influence on the sign. The effects of the five elements on the Ox are described below, together with the years in which the elements were exercising their influence. Therefore all Oxen born in 1901 and 1961 are Metal Oxen, those born in 1913 and 1973 are Water Oxen, and so on.

Metal Ox: 1901, 1961
This Ox is confident and very strong-willed. He can be blunt and forthright in his views and is not afraid of speaking his mind. He sets about his objectives with a dogged determination, but he can become so wrapped up in his various activities that he can be oblivious to the thoughts and feelings of those around him, and this can sometimes be to his detriment. He is honest and dependable and will never promise more than he can deliver. He has a good appreciation of the arts and usually has a small circle of very good and loyal friends.

Water Ox: 1913, 1973
This Ox has a sharp and penetrating mind. He is a good organizer and sets about his work in a methodical manner. He is not as narrow-minded as some of the other types of Oxen and is more willing to involve others in his plans and aspirations. He usually has very high moral standards and is often attracted to careers in public service. He is a good judge of character and has such a friendly and persuasive manner that he usually experiences little difficulty in securing his objectives. He is popular and has an excellent way with children.

Wood Ox: 1925, 1985
The Wood Ox conducts himself with an air of dignity and authority and will often take a leading role in any enterprise

in which he gets involved. He is very self-confident and is direct in his dealings with others. He does, however, have a quick temper and has no hesitation in speaking his mind. He has tremendous drive and will-power and has an extremely good memory. The Wood Ox is particularly loyal and devoted to the members of his family and has a most caring nature.

Fire Ox: 1937
The Fire Ox has a powerful and assertive personality and is a hard and conscientious worker. He holds strong views and has very little patience when things do not go his own way. He can also get carried away in the excitement of the moment and does not always take into account the views of those around him. He nevertheless has many leadership qualities and will often reach positions of power, eminence and wealth. He usually has a small group of loyal and close friends and is very devoted to his family.

Earth Ox: 1949
This Ox sets about everything he does in a sensible and level-headed manner. He is ambitious, but he is also realistic in his aims and is often prepared to work long hours in order to secure his objectives. He is shrewd in financial and business matters and is a very good judge of character. He has a quiet nature and is greatly admired for his sincerity and integrity. He is also very loyal to his family and friends and his views and opinions are often sought by others.

Prospects for the Ox in 1994

The Chinese New Year starts on 10 February 1994. Until then, the old year, the Year of the Rooster, is still making its presence felt.

The Year of the Rooster (23 January 1993 to 9 February 1994) will have been an important and constructive year for the Ox. He is likely to have made significant progress in many of his activities as well as having led a generally enjoyable domestic and social life.

For what remains of the Rooster year, the Ox should continue to look for opportunities to promote his skills and talents. He should be bold and determined, and if he sees any openings that interest him, particularly involving his work, he should not hesitate to follow them up. The Rooster year is a year for experimenting, for promoting ideas and for pushing forward with objectives, and the progress the Ox can make in the closing stages of the year can, with the right attitude, be quite considerable.

However, despite the generally positive trends, the Ox does need to exercise care when dealing with money matters. He would do well not to enter into any risky or speculative undertakings at this time or to be too lavish with his spending. If he takes risks, he could easily end up the loser.

The Ox will lead a pleasing social life during the Rooster year and any Ox who may have been lonely in recent times will have a very good chance to establish some new and meaningful friendships in the closing months of the year. The Ox will be much in demand with his family and friends over the Christmas and New Year holidays and he is likely to attend some most pleasant social gatherings at this time. He would also do well to try and contact some friends he has not heard from recently. They may have some interesting news for him!

However, in view of all the pressures and demands that the Ox will have experienced in the Rooster year, he would do well to set some time aside to rest and unwind. Although he is usually blessed with considerable stamina, the demands of the year will have taken a lot out of him and he will feel considerably revitalized if he gives himself the opportunity to relax.

The Year of the Dog starts on 10 February 1994 and will be a varied year for the Ox. He can look forward to making progress in many aspects of his life, but this progress will not be without effort on his part.

In work matters, the Ox would do well to continue to set about his activities in his own methodical and conscientious way. There will be obstacles to some of the things that he wishes to accomplish and he may find some of his colleagues are at times awkward, but providing the Ox perseveres and concentrates on doing what he thinks is right, his efforts will be rewarded. In 1994 the Ox needs to exercise patience, tact and perseverance. Providing he does this, he will be able to make progress. He will also find that if he should experience a set-back, a new opportunity could arise out of that reversal and he should not be too discouraged by any initial opposition that he faces. Provided he continues to act in a way that he thinks is right and looks for ways round any problems that might occur, he will do well. Also, if he meets with any opposition to his ideas and plans, he will get better results by compromise rather than confrontation. To remain stubborn and intransigent could only make matters worse for him. This is a point all Oxen should bear in mind.

Those Oxen seeking work should pursue any opportunities that they see and remain determined and persistent. Admittedly there may be disappointments and moments of despair, but the Ox is well known for his tenacity and, by persevering, many Oxen will be successful in gaining another position during the year. It may also be helpful for the Ox to consider lines of work which he may not have contemplated before – the year could contain a few pleasant surprises for the Ox and a change in the type of work that he does might be one of them. He could well feel stimulated by a new challenge and the opportunities that this can bring.

The Ox will see a general improvement in his finances over the year and, while he still needs to keep a watch over his outgoings, he will end the year in a more secure financial position than he enjoyed at the beginning of the year. He could also be fortunate in some large purchases that he makes and, by looking around, could obtain some very worthwhile bargains, particularly items for himself and for his home.

Many Oxen will also carry out alterations to their accommodation over the year and generally the improvements will go well. However, Oxen who intend to move should check all the paperwork and costs involved very carefully. Inattention to details could cause unnecessary problems and additional expense.

The Ox will lead a pleasant domestic life over the year. His family and friends will be most supportive and the Ox should remember that if he has any matter that is causing him concern, he should seek the advice of those around him. Some Oxen may themselves have to support and assist someone with difficulties to overcome, and in such a case the Ox's patient and understanding manner will do much to help.

The Ox will also lead a busy social life over the year – for some Oxen, it may even be busier than they like or are accustomed to! However, the social occasions that the Ox attends will enable him broaden his circle of acquaintances and while he may not appreciate it at the time, the contacts that he makes now could prove of some value to him in the future. The Year of the Dog is a particularly good year for romance and also for the Ox to get married.

Travel is well aspected in 1994 and there will be opportunities for the Ox to visit places which he may have longed to see for some time or to visit distant relations. The Ox will also benefit from any short breaks or week-ends away that he can take over the year. To drive himself too hard without giving himself a proper break could leave him prone to ailments associated with stress and strain. The Ox will also be helped if he sets some regular time aside to devote to his interests and recreational pursuits. If he does not get much exercise during the day, some additional walking, swimming or a suitable sporting activity could do much to improve his well-being.

Generally 1994 will be an important and ultimately satisfying year for the Ox. Admittedly, he may not have things all his own way, but in dealing with any problems that do occur in a positive and constructive manner, he can turn set-backs to his advantage, create new opportunities and win the respect of others. Indeed, it is through his strength and resolve that he will be able to make steady progress, particularly in the second half of the year.

As far as the different types of Ox are concerned, 1994 will be an important but demanding year for the **Metal Ox**. To get the best results from the year, he needs to pay careful attention to the views of others and to make sure that he has support before making any important decisions or undertaking new ventures. This is a year for joint rather than independent action and the Metal Ox, who is sometimes reserved and independent, does need to bear this in mind at all times. Also he can occasionally be stubborn and this is a trait that he does need to watch over the year. To go against the wishes of others or to be uncooperative in a certain matter could cause problems in his relations with others and impede his progress. This can be a positive and fulfilling year for the Metal Ox but he does need to act in unison with others and handle his relations with those around him with tact and care. He should also remember that if he has any awkward problem to deal with, those around him will be ready to advise him and in 1994 all Metal Oxen will greatly benefit from the advice, support and encouragement they are given. The Metal Ox can make steady progress in his work over the year and many can look forward to promotion or a new job in the latter part of 1994. The Metal Ox will lead a busy but enjoyable social and domestic life over the year and the summer months are likely to be a particularly favourable time for him.

Although not all the events of the year will work out as

well as the **Water Ox** may hope, 1994 will still be an important and generally satisfying year for him. He may find that some of his plans and hopes for the year will meet with opposition or delay, but by perseverance, determination and persuasion, he can achieve much. By facing up to any difficulties or problems that occur, he will grow in stature and self-confidence, and the experience he gains and the respect that he earns from others will be very much to his future advantage. So while not everything that occurs in 1994 will be without difficulty, the Water Ox's gains can still be considerable, both in terms of experience and in the results he obtains in the latter part of the year. It is then that the Water Ox will begin to see the fruits of his labours and can make significant progress. The Water Ox is also likely to see some important changes in his work and many will be successful in obtaining a new and more responsible position. Also if he is able to increase his skills over the year this will be to his future advantage. The year will, however, prove quite expensive for the Water Ox and it would be in his interests to keep a watch on his general level of outgoings. He will lead an enjoyable social life in 1994 as well as having the opportunity to travel, but both could prove a drain on his resources. The year is very well aspected for romance and for making new friends and many Water Oxen will marry over the year or meet their future partner.

This will be a quiet but pleasant year for the **Wood Ox**. He will be much in demand with his family and friends and his social life will be busier than it has been in recent years. Indeed, if the Wood Ox is seeking new friends or wants to broaden his circle of acquaintances, this would be an ideal year for him to go out more, join local societies and attend more social functions. The Wood Ox's family will also be particularly important to him over the year. They will support him if he has any difficulties to overcome and any assistance and advice he himself can give to his loved ones will be thoroughly appreciated. There will be opportunities for travel over the year and a holiday taken in the late summer could prove especially enjoyable. Generally 1994 will be a favourable year for the Wood Ox, but he could encounter problems if he becomes over-ambitious in the things that he attempts. Throughout the year he should try to spread his activities out. He will also find that he will obtain greater success and more satisfaction by devoting his energies to areas which are familiar to him rather than involving himself in new and ambitious ventures. If he has any problems, particularly of a bureaucratic nature, he would do well to seek the advice of others rather than tackle the problem single-handedly and possibly causing himself much needless worry and anxiety.

This will be an interesting year for the **Fire Ox**, and over the course of the year he could see a number of changes taking place. These could involve his work, his accommodation or his personal situation. Out of these changes will come new opportunities and interesting challenges – challenges which can motivate and stimulate the Fire Ox into improving his present situation. In some respects 1994 can be seen as the start of a new chapter in his life. Admittedly not all the changes that occur will be to the Fire Ox's liking and some of the year could be unsettling, but a new and important phase of his life is about to begin and given his many talents and capabilities, he can turn this phase into a most positive and fulfilling one. As far as possible, the Fire Ox should be open in discussing his plans and hopes with his loved ones and bear in mind their thoughts before embarking on any new and major undertaking. The Fire Ox should also be realistic in his objectives over the year. Despite his enthusiasm and good intentions, he cannot achieve all his ambitions at the same time. This year is for planning, for consultation and then, latterly, for action. In view of the busy nature of the year, it is also important that the Fire Ox does not neglect his own well-being. He should exercise well, eat a healthy diet and also make sure that he sets time aside both for his family and his own recreational interests. A few breaks taken at different intervals of the year could prove most beneficial for him.

This will be a quiet and generally satisfying year for the **Earth Ox**. He will make steady progress in most of his activities and while he may not accomplish all that he had hoped over the year, he will still be pleased with his accomplishments. He should continue to set about his work and various activities in his usual methodical way but should be wary of over-committing himself or of starting new ventures without the proper preparation. He would also do well to give some thought to his future and if he is able to add to his skills in any way he will find that this will be of considerable value to him over the next few years. This will, in many respects, be a year of consolidation and planning for the future. The experience he gains and the plans that he makes will help to pave the way for the Earth Ox's future success. As with all Oxen, the Earth Ox may have a few problems to overcome during the year and these could occur in almost any aspect of his life. In dealing with these problems he should endeavour to look for compromise rather than confrontation and seek the opinion of others rather than shouldering any worries he might have single-handed. Fortunately, any problems that do arise are not likely to be serious and will not spoil what will be a generally pleasant year for him. The Earth Ox can look forward to a content social and domestic life over the year and many will have good cause for a family celebration. Although 1994 will not be a bad year financially for him, it would still be in his interests to keep a watch on his general level of expenditure. His outgoings could be greater than he thought and he may also find it helpful to conduct a review of his outgoings and financial commitments. He will be surprised at the difference a few alterations can make.

Famous Oxen

Hans Christian Andersen, Johann Sebastian Bach, Warren Beatty, Tony Benn, Chuck Berry, Jon Bon Jovi, Willy Brandt, Jeff Bridges, Benjamin Britten, Frank Bruno, Richard Burton, Barbara Bush, Johnny Carson, Barbara Cartland, Judith Chalmers, Charlie Chaplin, Warren Christopher, George Cole, Peter Cook, Bill Cosby, Tony Curtis, Sammy Davis Jr, Jacques Delors, Walt Disney, Patrick Duffy, Harry Enfield, Jane Fonda, Michael Foot, Gerald Ford, Edward Fox, Michael J. Fox, Peter Gabriel, Handel, King Harald V of Norway, Robert Hardy, Charles Haughey, Nigel Havers, Adolf Hitler, Dustin Hoffman, Anthony Hopkins, Billy Joel, Don Johnson, Jack Jones, King Juan Carlos of Spain, Mark Knopfler, Burt Lancaster, Jessica Lange, Angela Lansbury, Jack Lemmon, Nicholas Lyndhurst, John MacGregor, Barry McGuigan, David Mellor, Warren Mitchell, Eddie Murphy, Napoleon, Pandit Nehru, Paul Newman, Jack Nicholson, Oscar Peterson, Colin Powell, Robert Redford, Rubens, Ian Rush, Willie Rushton, Arthur Scargill, Monica Seles, Peter Sellers, Jean Sibelius, Valerie Singleton, Jimmy Somerville, Sissy Spacek, Bruce Springsteen, Rod Steiger, Meryl Streep, Loretta Swit, Lady Thatcher, Twiggy, Mary Tyler Moore, Dick Van Dyke, the Princess of Wales, the Duke of Wellington, Alan Whicker, Ernie Wise, W.B. Yeats.

The Tiger

8 February 1902 to	28 January 1903	*Water Tiger*
26 January 1914 to	13 February 1915	*Wood Tiger*
13 February 1926 to	1 February 1927	*Fire Tiger*
31 January 1938 to	18 February 1939	*Earth Tiger*
17 February 1950 to	5 February 1951	*Metal Tiger*
5 February 1962 to	24 January 1963	*Water Tiger*
23 January 1974 to	10 February 1975	*Wood Tiger*
9 February 1986 to	28 January 1987	*Fire Tiger*

The Personality of the Tiger

I'm sure you have a theme: the theme of life. You can embellish it or desecrate it, but it's your theme, and as long as you follow it, you will experience harmony and peace of mind.

– *Agatha Christie: a Tiger.*

The Tiger is born under the sign of courage. He is a charismatic figure and usually holds very firm views and beliefs. He is strong-willed and determined, and sets about most of the things he does with a tremendous energy and enthusiasm. He is very alert and quick-witted and his mind is forever active. He is a highly original thinker and is nearly always brimming with new ideas or full of enthusiasm for some new project or scheme.

The Tiger adores challenges and he loves to get involved in anything which he thinks has an exciting future or which catches his imagination. He is prepared to take risks and does not like to be bound either by convention or the dictates of others. The Tiger likes to be free to act as he chooses and at least once during his life he will throw caution to the wind and go off and do the things he wants to do.

The Tiger does, however, have a somewhat restless nature. Even though he is often prepared to throw himself wholeheartedly into a project, his initial enthusiasm can soon wane if he sees something more appealing. He can also be rather impulsive and there will have been occasions in his life when he has acted in a manner which he has later regretted. If the Tiger were to think things out or to persevere in his various activities, he would almost certainly enjoy a greater degree of success than he would otherwise obtain.

Fortunately the Tiger is lucky in most of his enterprises, but should things not work out as he had hoped, he is liable to suffer from severe bouts of depression and it will often take him a long time to recover. The Tiger's life often consists of a series of ups and downs.

The Tiger is, however, very adaptable. He has an adventurous spirit and rarely stays in the same place for long. In the early stages of his life he is likely to try his hand at several different jobs and he will also change his residence fairly frequently.

The Tiger is very honest and open in his dealings with others. He hates any sort of hypocrisy or falsehood. He is also well known for being blunt and forthright and has no hesitation in speaking his mind. He can also be most rebellious at times, particularly against any form of petty authority, and while this can lead the Tiger into conflict with others, he is never one to shrink from an argument or avoid standing up for what he believes is right.

The Tiger is a natural leader and can invariably rise to the top of his chosen profession. He does not, however, care for anything too bureaucratic or detailed and he also does

THE TIGER

not like to obey orders. He can be stubborn and obstinate and throughout his life he likes to retain a certain amount of independence in his actions and be responsible to no one but himself. He likes to consider that all his achievements are due to his own efforts, and unless he cannot avoid it he will rarely ask for support from others.

Ironically, despite his self-confidence and leadership qualities, the Tiger can be indecisive and will often delay making a major decision until the very last moment. He can also be sensitive to criticism.

Although the Tiger is capable of earning large sums of money, he is rather a spendthrift and does not always put his money to its best use. He can also be most generous and will often shower lavish gifts on friends and relations.

The Tiger cares very much for his reputation and the image that he tries to project. He carries himself with an air of dignity and authority and enjoys being the centre of attention. He is very adept at attracting publicity, both for himself and for the causes which he supports.

The Tiger often marries young and he will find himself best suited to those born under the signs of the Pig, Dog, Horse and Goat. He can also get on well with the Rat, Rabbit and Rooster, but will find the Ox and Snake a bit too quiet and too serious for his liking, and he will also be highly irritated by the Monkey's rather mischievous and inquisitive ways. The Tiger will also find it difficult to get on with another Tiger or a Dragon – both partners will want to dominate the relationship and could find it difficult to compromise on even the smallest of matters.

The Tigress is lively, witty and a marvellous hostess at parties. She is usually most attractive and takes great care over her appearance. She can also be a very doting mother and while she believes in letting her children have their freedom, she makes an excellent teacher and will ensure that her children are brought up well and want for nothing. Like her male counterpart, she has numerous interests and likes to have sufficient independence and freedom to go off and do the things that she wants to do. She also has a most caring and generous nature.

The Tiger has many commendable qualities. He is honest, courageous and often a source of inspiration for others. Providing he can curb the wilder excesses of his restless nature, he is almost certain to lead a most fulfilling and satisfying life.

The Five Different Types of Tiger

In addition to the 12 signs of the Chinese zodiac, there are five elements and these have a strengthening or moderating influence on the sign. The effects of the five elements on the Tiger are described below, together with the years in which the elements were exercising their influence. Therefore all Tigers born in 1950 are Metal Tigers, those born in 1902 and 1962 are Water Tigers and so on.

Metal Tiger: 1950
The Metal Tiger has an assertive and outgoing personality. He is very ambitious and, while his aims may change from time to time, he will work relentlessly until he has obtained what he wants. He can, however, be impatient for results and also get highly strung if things do not work out as he would like. He is distinctive in his appearance and is admired and respected by many.

Water Tiger: 1902, 1962
This Tiger has a wide variety of interests and is always eager to experiment with new ideas or go off and explore distant lands. He is versatile, shrewd and has a kindly nature. The Water Tiger tends to remain calm in a crisis, although he can be annoyingly indecisive at times. He communicates well with others and through his many capabilities and persuasive nature he usually achieves what he wants in life. He is also highly imaginative and is often a gifted orator or writer.

Wood Tiger: 1914, 1974
The Wood Tiger has a very friendly and pleasant personality. He is less independent than some of the other types of Tiger and is more prepared to work with others to secure a desired objective. However, he does have a tendency to jump from one thing to another and can get easily distracted. He is usually very popular, has a large circle of friends and invariably leads a busy and enjoyable social life. He also has a good sense of humour.

Fire Tiger: 1926, 1986
The Fire Tiger sets about everything he does with great verve and enthusiasm. He loves action and is always ready to throw himself wholeheartedly into anything which catches his imagination. He has many leadership qualities and is capable of communicating his ideas and enthusiasm to others. He is very much an optimist and can be most generous. He has a likeable nature and can be a witty and persuasive speaker.

Earth Tiger: 1938
This Tiger is responsible and level-headed. He studies everything objectively and tries to be scrupulously fair in all his dealings. Unlike other Tigers, he is prepared to specialize in certain areas rather than get distracted by other matters, but he can become so involved with what he is doing that he does not always take into account the views and opinions of those around him. He has good business sense and is usually very successful in later life. He has a large circle of friends and pays great attention to both his appearance and his reputation.

Prospects for the Tiger in 1994

The Chinese New Year starts on 10 February 1994. Until then, the old year, the Year of the Rooster, is still making its presence felt.

The Year of the Rooster (23 January 1993 to 9 February 1994) is likely to have been a constructive year for the Tiger and the experience that he will have gained will serve him well in the future. For what remains of the Rooster year, the Tiger should continue to set about his activities in his usual diligent and enterprising way. He should remain alert for new opportunities to pursue, especially in November 1993 and January 1994, but at the same time be mindful of the views of those around him. In all his undertakings, the Tiger cannot afford to remain independent or to ignore the feelings of others. If he does, he will find progress more difficult and his relations with others could become strained. This is a time for concerted rather than independent action.

The Tiger is likely to receive some encouraging news concerning his work and prospects towards the end of the Rooster year and if he can go on any courses or add to his skills at this time, he will find that this will be very much to his future advantage. He will also be helped by giving some thought to what he would like to achieve in the forthcoming year and by discussing his plans and ideas with those around him.

The Tiger will be fortunate in money matters in the closing stages of the Rooster year. However, he may find the expenses he incurs around the Christmas and New Year holidays, together with the socializing he undertakes, will be far more than he anticipated. The Tiger is, though, likely to have a most enjoyable time over the holiday period as well as being able to unwind after the strains and stresses of the Rooster year. He will also be able to look forward to the promising times that lie ahead for him in the Chinese New Year.

The Year of the Dog starts on 10 February 1994 and is going to be a satisfying and fulfilling year for the Tiger. If, in recent years, he has felt that he has not been realizing his full potential or that his efforts have not been obtaining the results they deserve, this will change in 1994. During the year the Tiger will notice an upturn in his fortunes, although how great an upturn this is is partly dependent upon the Tiger himself.

To achieve success and to take advantage of the favourable trends that prevail, the Tiger needs to work hard, remain persistent and be positive in his outlook. Over the year he will find much truth in the proverb 'As ye shall sow, so shall ye reap.' By making an effort and by going after particular objectives, the Tiger can achieve great success. But if he is not prepared to make the effort, gets distracted easily or wastes his energies by committing himself to too many activities, then his results will be much more limited. In 1994 the Tiger must remain dedicated to a few specific objectives and work purposefully towards those objectives. If he does, then this will be a truly splendid year for him.

The Tiger can do particularly well in his work. He will greatly impress others with his warm and friendly personality and will win ready support for his plans and ideas. In view of these favourable trends, many Tigers will be promoted during the year or can look forward to being given more challenging duties. Also, those Tigers seeking work could be successful in obtaining a new position and should remain alert for opportunities to pursue, particularly in the early stages of the year.

The Tiger will be generally fortunate in money matters and any Tiger who has been experiencing financial problems will find his situation eased over the year. However, it would still be in his interests to keep a close watch over his general level of expenditure. He can at times be rather extravagant in his spending and if he can curb this tendency, he could find that any savings he can make will be useful later. If he is able to start a savings scheme or take out a policy which would make provision for him in the future he could find this will prove a valuable asset in years to come.

The Tiger can look forward to leading an enjoyable domestic and social life over the year. He will find his family and friends most supportive and, as far as possible, he should actively involve those around him in his various activities. He will be considerably helped by the encouragement and advice that they give him over the year.

Socially, too, this will be a busy year for the Tiger and he can look forward to attending some very pleasant functions. His circle of friends and acquaintances is also likely to increase and for those Tigers who are unattached, the summer months could prove a particularly happy time.

The year will prove quite busy for the Tiger and it is important that he does set some time aside for his hobbies and interests. Outdoor activities are particularly well aspected and the Tiger will also be able to indulge in his love of travel over the year. Many Tigers will travel considerable distances in 1994 and their journeys will prove interesting and enjoyable, especially if they visit areas that are new to them.

Naturally no year is without its problems and there are certain areas that the Tiger will need to watch. In 1994 he cannot afford to neglect his own well-being. Sometimes he drives himself too hard and puts himself under unnecessary pressure and strain. Although he does want to do well – and *will* do well in 1994 – it is important that he spreads his activities and commitments out over the year. He also would do well to set a regular time aside to relax and unwind and to devote to recreational pursuits. Although the Tiger is blessed with much vitality, even he needs quiet periods to rest and restore his energy. If he relies a lot on fast and convenience foods he will find that a few modifications to his diet will be in his interests and all Tigers will benefit by taking that little extra care of themselves over the year. By taking regular exercise and eating a healthy and balanced diet the Tiger will feel considerably better in himself.

The other area that could cause problems this year is the Tiger's relations with others. Although he can look forward to receiving valuable support over the year, there is a danger that he could jeopardize this by speaking his mind too freely or being intransigent over some matter. In 1994 the Tiger does need to exercise diplomacy and tact in his dealing with others and be ready to compromise in any awkward or difficult situation. Provided he bears this in mind, he will win the respect and support of others and this will help him in this important and successful year.

Generally 1994 is a positive year for the Tiger and by going after clear objectives and working hard, he can do well. The opportunities for advancement are there and it rests with the Tiger to turn these favourable aspects to his advantage.

As far as the different types of Tiger are concerned, 1994 will be a busy and demanding year for the **Metal Tiger**. He can look forward to doing well in business and financial matters, and will win ready support for his plans and ideas. Indeed, 1994 is very much a year for the Metal Tiger to pursue his aims and ambitions with his usual solid determination. It is a time for being bold, for putting past set-backs behind him and seizing the initiative. There will be plenty of opportunities for the Metal Tiger to improve upon his position over the year and he should make the most of the positive trends that prevail. Admittedly, not all the events will be entirely in his favour, but by overcoming any problems that do occur effectively and without rancour, he will win the respect of others and could even turn a set-back or disappointment to his advantage. While he is likely to make considerable progress in his work, however, he should not become so preoccupied with his own activities that he neglects his home and social life. He should involve himself in the interests of his loved ones and although he may at times feel under pressure, it is important that he sets some time aside for recreational activities. He could find several short breaks taken at different intervals throughout the year particularly beneficial. Many Metal Tigers will take great pride and pleasure in the successes enjoyed by a close relation over the year and any encouragement and support that the Metal Tiger can give to a younger relative will be greatly appreciated.

This will be an important year for the **Water Tiger**, and over the year he will see several changes taking place. This could involve moving to a new area or taking on new responsibilities at work. While any changes that do occur may, at the time, seem daunting, events will work out in the Water Tiger's favour. A new job or change in the nature of his work will enable him to acquire additional skills and this in itself will enhance his future prospects. He will also find any changes that occur, whether in his work or accommodation, will bring new opportunities for him. The challenges that the year will offer will be stimulating as well as providing an added impetus to do well. In addition to the progress he will make, the Water Tiger will also be sowing the seeds for further advances. He will be fortunate in financial matters and many Water Tigers can also look forward to receiving a sum of money from an unexpected source over the year. The Water Tiger's domestic and social life will be most pleasurable, although he may have to assist an older relation who has a difficult problem to overcome. His calm and objective nature will do much to help the situation. The Water Tiger will take great delight in outdoor pursuits and those who enjoy travel, sport or activities such as walking and gardening will find these interests particularly pleasurable.

This will be a positive but challenging year for the **Wood Tiger**. Some aspects of his life will go extremely well for him, but there will be other areas in which he could face difficulties. However, these problems are unlikely to be serious and in some respects could even work out to his advantage. Any problems that do arise could help to focus the Wood Tiger's attention on his present situation and make him review and possibly strengthen his plans. Throughout the year he should act with resolution and be determined to make the most of his considerable capabilities. In many respects the work and experience that the Wood Tiger obtains over the year will help to lay the foundations for the positive advances he will make in the next few years. Over the year the Wood Tiger will not only gain much valuable experience, but will grow in stature and self-confidence as well as rising in the esteem of others. This will be a year of development and also a time when the Wood Tiger needs to consider the direction that he would like his life to take over the next few years. The decisions and actions that he takes in 1994 will be both important and far-reaching, but he can take comfort from the knowledge that those around him have his best interests at heart and will give him helpful and constructive advice should he ask. As well as possible changes in his work and accommodation, the Wood Tiger will also see changes in his personal life this year. Some Wood Tigers will get married, some will see an addition to their family or some may decide to travel extensively over the year. This will be an eventful year for the Wood Tiger and he will emerge from it a much stronger and wiser person. The decisions and actions that he will take will contribute to his progress in the next few years.

This will be a pleasant year for the **Fire Tiger**. He can look forward to having some most enjoyable times with his family and friends and those around him will give him ready support and encouragement for his various activities. His social life in particular will give him much pleasure and he is likely to make some new and good friends over the year. However, while the aspects are generally favourable for the Fire Tiger, he may still have a few problems to contend with. These are more likely to be nigglesome than serious, but could arise out of a misunderstanding with someone or a bureaucratic matter. In either case, the Fire Tiger would do well to sort any problem out as quickly as he can, preferably with the support and assistance of others. To deal with any difficulty on his own will not only put him under increased pressure but could also prolong the situation unnecessarily. The Fire Tiger has many good friends he can call upon to advise and assist him, and he should not hesitate to avail himself of the help they can offer. The Fire Tiger should bear in mind that throughout the year forms and official paperwork do need careful handling and he would do well to check the implications of any important document or agreement that he has to sign. On a more positive note, the Fire Tiger will obtain a lot of enjoyment from his various interests and especially from outdoor activities. Travel is well aspected and a holiday or short break taken in the spring is likely to be particularly memorable.

This will be an interesting and varied year for the **Earth Tiger**. He can look forward to making progress in many of his activities, although he may have to show a certain amount of flexibility in his plans. He could find that in the Year of the Dog even the best laid plans go awry and that not everything will turn out exactly as he had intended. However, while some of the events that happen may give rise to moments of uncertainty and frustration, the Earth Tiger is not one who is defeated easily and he will be able to overcome any problems that arise. He will also find that some of the changes that occur, whether in his work or accommodation, will be to his long-term advantage and will give rise to new and brighter opportunities. However, throughout the year he does need to be flexible in his outlook and be ready to adapt to new situations. If he can do this, this will be a very good and constructive year for him. The Earth Tiger will lead a generally happy social and domestic life in 1994 and will do well in financial matters. He will also obtain considerable pleasure from a new interest that he takes up and he could find that an activity such as photography, learning a musical instrument, painting or writing will give him much satisfaction in this and future years.

Famous Tigers

Les Aspin, Sir David Attenborough, Bruce Babbitt, Queen Beatrix of the Netherlands, Beethoven, Chuck Berry, Richard Branson, Mel Brooks, Isambard Kingdom Brunel, Simon Cadell, Tommy Cannon, Agatha Christie, James Clavell, David Coleman, Phil Collins, Jason Connery, Alan Coren, Tom Cruise, Paul Daniels, Emily Dickinson, David Dimbleby, Isadora Duncan, Dwight Eisenhower, Queen Elizabeth II, Frederick Forsyth, Jodie Foster, Connie Francis, Charles de Gaulle, Crystal Gayle, Susan George, Mel Gibson, Goya, Sir Alec Guinness, Bryan Gould, Elliott Gould, Lord Howe, William Hurt, Derek Jacobi, David Jacobs, Caron Keating, Matthew Kelly, Sarah Kennedy, Stan Laurel, Ian McCaskill, Ramsay Macdonald, Karl Marx, Marilyn Monroe, Eric Morecambe, Rudolph Nureyev, Lord Owen, Paganini, Jonathan Porritt, Marco Polo, John Prescott, the Princess Royal, Suzi Quatro, Diana Rigg, Lionel Ritchie, Kenny Rogers, Sir Jimmy Savile, Phillip Schofield, John Smith (MP), Sir David Steel, Pamela Stephenson, Dame Joan Sutherland, Dylan Thomas, Liv Ullman, Julie Walters, Oscar Wilde, Terry Wogan, Stevie Wonder.

The Rabbit

29 January 1903	to	15 February 1904	***Water Rabbit***
14 February 1915	to	2 February 1916	***Wood Rabbit***
2 February 1927	to	22 January 1928	***Fire Rabbit***
19 February 1939	to	7 February 1940	***Earth Rabbit***
6 February 1951	to	26 January 1952	***Metal Rabbit***
25 January 1963	to	12 February 1964	***Water Rabbit***
11 February 1975	to	30 January 1976	***Wood Rabbit***
29 January 1987	to	16 February 1988	***Fire Rabbit***

The Personality of the Rabbit

Wondrous is the strength of cheerfulness, and its power of endurance – the cheerful man will do more in the same time, will do it better, will persevere in it longer than the sad or sullen.

– Thomas Carlyle: a Rabbit.

The Rabbit is born under the signs of virtue and prudence. He is intelligent, well-mannered, and prefers a quiet and peaceful existence. He dislikes any sort of unpleasantness and will try to steer clear of arguments and disputes. He is very much a pacifist and tends to have a calming influence on those around him.

He has wide interests and usually has a good appreciation of the arts and the finer things in life. He also knows how to enjoy himself and will often gravitate to the best restaurants and night spots in town.

The Rabbit is a witty and intelligent speaker and loves being involved in a good discussion. His views and advice are often sought by others and he can be relied upon to be discreet and diplomatic. He will rarely raise his voice in anger and will even turn a blind eye to matters which displease him just to preserve the peace. The Rabbit likes to remain on good terms with everyone, but he can be rather sensitive and takes any form of criticism very badly. He will also be the first to get out of the way if he sees any form of trouble brewing.

The Rabbit is a quiet and efficient worker and has an extremely good memory. He is very astute in business and financial matters, but his degree of success often depends on the conditions that prevail. He hates being in a situation which is fraught with tension or where he has to make quick and sudden decisions. Wherever possible he will plan his various activities with the utmost care and a good deal of caution. He does not like to take risks and does not take kindly to changes. Basically, he seeks a secure, calm and stable environment, and when conditions are right he is more than happy to leave things as they are.

The Rabbit is conscientious in most of the things that he does and, because of his methodical and ever-watchful nature, he can often do well in his chosen profession. He makes a good diplomat, lawyer, shopkeeper, administrator or priest and he excels in any job where he can use his superb skills as a communicator. He tends to be loyal to his employers and is respected for his integrity and honesty, but if the Rabbit ever finds himself in a position of great power he can become rather intransigent and authoritarian.

The Rabbit attaches great importance to his home and will often spend much time and money to maintain and furnish it and to fit it with all the latest comforts – the Rabbit is very much a creature of comfort! He is also something of a collector and there are many Rabbits who derive much pleasure from collecting antiques, stamps, coins, *objets d'art* or anything else which catches their eye or particularly interests them.

The female Rabbit has a friendly, caring and considerate nature, and will do all in her power to give her home a happy and loving atmosphere. She is also very sociable and enjoys holding parties and entertaining. She has a great ability to make the maximum use of her time and, although she involves herself in numerous activities, she always manages to find time to sit back and enjoy a good read or a chat. She has a great sense of humour, is very artistic and is often a talented gardener.

The Rabbit takes considerable care over his appearance and is usually smart and very well turned out. He also attaches great importance to his relations with others and matters of the heart are particularly important to him. He will rarely be short of admirers and will often have several serious romances before he settles down. The Rabbit is not the most faithful of signs, but he will find that he is especially well-suited to those born under the signs of the Goat, Snake, Pig and Ox. Due to his sociable and easy-going manner he can also get on well with the Tiger, Dragon, Horse, Monkey, Dog and another Rabbit, but the Rabbit will feel ill-at-ease with the Rat and Rooster as both these signs tend to speak their mind and be critical in their comments, and the Rabbit just loathes any form of criticism or unpleasantness.

The Rabbit is usually lucky in life and often has the happy knack of being in the right place at the right time. He is talented and quick-witted, but he does sometimes put pleasure before work, and wherever possible will tend to opt for the easy life. He can at times be a little reserved and suspicious of the motives of others, but generally the Rabbit will lead a long and contented life and one which – as far as possible – will be free of strife and discord.

The Five Different Types of Rabbit

In addition to the 12 signs of the Chinese zodiac, there are five elements and these have a strengthening or moderating influence on the sign. The effects of the five elements on the Rabbit are described below, together with the years in which the elements were exercising their influence. Therefore all Rabbits born in 1951 are Metal Rabbits, those born in 1903 and 1963 are Water Rabbits, and so on.

Metal Rabbit: 1951
This Rabbit is capable, ambitious and has very definite views on what he wants to achieve in life. He can occasionally appear reserved and aloof, but this is mainly because he likes to keep his thoughts and ideas to himself. He has a very quick and alert mind and is particularly shrewd in business matters. He can also be very cunning in his actions. The Metal Rabbit has a good appreciation of the arts and likes to mix in the best circles. He usually has a small but very loyal group of friends.

Water Rabbit: 1903, 1963
The Water Rabbit is popular, intuitive and keenly aware of the feelings of those around him. He can, however, be rather sensitive and tends to take things too much to heart. He is very precise and thorough in everything he does and has an exceedingly good memory. He tends to be quiet and at times rather withdrawn, but he expresses his ideas well and is highly regarded by his family, friends and colleagues.

Wood Rabbit: 1915, 1975
The Wood Rabbit is likeable, easy going and very adaptable. He prefers to work in groups rather than on his own and likes to have the support and encouragement of others. He can, however, be rather reticent in expressing his views and it would be in his own interests to become a little more open and forthright and let others know how he feels on

certain matters. He usually has many friends and enjoys an active social life. He is noted for his generosity.

Fire Rabbit: 1927, 1987
The Fire Rabbit has a friendly, outgoing personality. He likes socializing and being on good terms with everyone. He is discreet and diplomatic and has a very good understanding of human nature. He is also strong-willed, and provided he has the necessary backing and support he can go far in life. He does not, however, suffer adversity well and can become moody and depressed when things are not working out as he would like. The Fire Rabbit is very intuitive and there are some who are even noted for their psychic ability. The Fire Rabbit has a particularly good manner with children.

Earth Rabbit: 1939
The Earth Rabbit is a quiet individual, but he is nevertheless very shrewd and astute. He is realistic in his aims and is prepared to work long and hard in order to achieve his objectives. He has good business sense and is invariably lucky in financial matters. He also has a most persuasive manner and usually experiences little difficulty in getting others to fall in with his plans. He is held in very high esteem by his friends and colleagues and his views and opinions are often sought and highly valued.

Prospects for the Rabbit in 1994

The Chinese New Year starts on 10 February 1994. Until then, the old year, the Year of the Rooster, is still making its presence felt.

The Year of the Rooster (23 January 1993 to 9 February 1994) will have been a mixed year for the Rabbit. He could have faced several problems and not made as much progress as he would have liked. He could also have found his plans difficult to carry out and may have felt that his efforts over the year have only met with limited success. However the Rabbit can take heart. All Rabbits will see a steady upturn in their fortunes in the closing stages of the year, an upturn which will carry on in 1994.

For what remains of the Rooster year, the Rabbit should continue to set about his various activities in his usual diligent way. The work that he does and the way he conducts his activities will have an important bearing on the future and in many respects the Year of the Rooster is a year of preparation and experience – preparation and experience that will prove valuable to the Rabbit later.

In the remaining months of the Rooster year the Rabbit should pay careful attention to any important correspondence that he receives. A letter could contain information that will be most useful to him later. He would also do well to exercise care in his spending. Although he is usually most careful when dealing with financial matters, the Rooster year is not a year when the Rabbit can push his luck or resources too far, or take risks with his money.

On a more positive note, he will find his family and friends a great help at this time. He would do well to discuss his views and plans with others as well as throwing himself wholeheartedly into the activities of his family and those around him. Domestically and socially, this can be a most enjoyable and fulfilling time for him.

The Rabbit will also obtain much pleasure from his various hobbies and interests at the end of the Rooster year, and these will help him to rest and unwind from everyday pressures. If he does not have an interest that would give him an opportunity to unwind, he would do well to take one up. He will find it will not only give him many hours of pleasure but could also lead to new friendships.

The Year of the Dog starts on 10 February 1994 and will be a generally pleasing year for the Rabbit. He will be able to make progress in many of his activities and will find it easier to proceed with his plans than in recent years.

In some respects 1994 will represent the start of a new and positive phase in the Rabbit's life. However, to get the year off to a good start he would do well to deal with any outstanding matters or problems he might have, particularly those which might have caused him concern in recent times. This could include correspondence which perhaps he may not have attended to or sorting out a difference of opinion with someone. Admittedly, as a Rabbit, he may sometimes prefer to put awkward matters to one side rather than deal with them, especially as he hates being in tense or difficult situations, but anything positive and constructive that he can do will be worth his while. It would also enable him to concentrate on his current objectives rather than be impeded by any worries lingering in the background.

The Rabbit will also benefit from taking stock of his present position and setting himself some priorities for the year. Usually, as a methodical and well-organized person, he does have some idea of his objectives, but in this year he does need to give some serious thought to his immediate future. If he can make a list of his most important objectives for the year, he will find that this will give him something positive to aim for and, by the end of 1994, he should be well pleased with what he has achieved.

Over the year the Rabbit will lead a content and settled home life and his family and those around him will be supportive and co-operative. He can also look forward to being actively involved in several family celebrations which are likely to give him much pleasure.

His social life too will be enjoyable and he will find his circle of friends and contacts will increase substantially as the year progresses. Rabbits who may have been lonely in recent times or suffered some sadness should view 1994 as a new start and a year of opportunity. By going out more and attending social gatherings, they too will find some new and valuable friends. For unattached Rabbits, the year is highly favourable for romance.

The Rabbit will also do well in financial matters and any Rabbit who may have been experiencing financial problems will find that his situation will improve during the year. However, despite these generally favourable aspects, the Rabbit does still need to exercise care in his general level of spending. It would be helpful for him to conduct a review of his regular outgoings and make any modifications he feels necessary. He will be surprised at the difference just a few adjustments can make in improving his financial situation.

There will be opportunities for the Rabbit to progress in his work over the year and many Rabbits will be given new and more challenging positions. Those Rabbits seeking employment should remain alert for opportunities to pursue and, if possible, they should try to take part in any training courses that they may be eligible for. Anything that the Rabbit can do to broaden his skills will be to his future advantage.

However, despite these generally favourable trends in work matters, there are two points that the Rabbit needs to bear in mind. The first is that he must avoid being over-ambitious. This is more a year of steady rather than rapid progress and if he tries to take on too much at any one time or aim for unrealistic objectives he will encounter disappointment. The second point is that while the Rabbit is usually adept at handling his relations with others, this year he could find some of his colleagues may at times prove awkward. In such a situation, the Rabbit should be his usual tactful and diplomatic self and, if possible, get to the root cause of the problem. He will find that by doing this and taking positive action, the difficulty can soon be resolved.

The Rabbit will obtain much satisfaction from his various hobbies and interests over the year. It is a particularly favourable time for creative pursuits and those Rabbits interested in the arts would do well to further and promote their talents. Although the Rabbit is unlikely to travel too far in 1994, any journeys that he does undertake will go well.

Generally 1994 will be a favourable year for the Rabbit, although the amount he achieves is partly dependent on him having clear objectives to aim for. With a positive and determined attitude he can make considerable, if not outstanding, progress in many of his activities. He can look forward to some happy and enjoyable times with his family and friends and he could also see an improvement in his financial situation over the year.

As far as the different types of Rabbit are concerned, 1994 will be a generally satisfying year for the **Metal Rabbit**. He will make steady progress over the year, but perhaps more importantly he will win the respect of others, increase his circle of friends and widen his experience. All this will help his prospects in the future. In 1994 the Metal Rabbit should concentrate on consolidating his present position while remaining alert for opportunities to pursue and for ways in which he can use his considerable talents. The work that he carries out and the efforts he makes, while not necessarily being fully rewarded in 1994, will prove an important contribution to the success he will enjoy in the next few years. In many respects this is a year for planning, for making reasonable progress and for preparing for the greater advances the Metal Rabbit can look forward to making in the future. Many Metal Rabbits will be given increased responsibilities in their work over the year and those seeking employment will find their persistence will be rewarded – perhaps when they least expect it! The Metal Rabbit will also do well in financial matters over the year. He can look forward to leading a contented domestic life and will have many happy times with his family and friends. Socially, too, this will be an active year for him and he will be invited to several functions. The Metal Rabbit will also obtain much pleasure from a hobby that he has and if he has not already tried to contact others who share his hobby he would do well to do so, perhaps by joining a club or society. He will find that this will lead to making new friends as well as making the hobby or interest that much more satisfying for him.

This will be a quiet and generally settled year for the **Water Rabbit**. He will make steady progress in his work and, while he may not accomplish all that he had hoped during the year, he will still be pleased with what he is actually able to achieve. To get the most favourable results in 1994 the Water Rabbit should continue to work to the best of his abilities, pursue any opportunities that are of interest to him and, most importantly, be prepared to work in conjunction with others. This is a year for concerted rather than independent action and if the Water Rabbit disregards the views of others or is reticent about involving others in his plans, he will find progress much more difficult and problems emerging. So throughout the year the Water Rabbit should make every effort to involve those around him in his activities. He will also find that some stages of the year will be busy; if he feels under pressure at any time he should not hesitate to ask for assistance from those around him. The Water Rabbit can look forward, however, to having some happy and memorable times with his family and friends. He could also have good cause for a personal celebration over the year and will take great delight in the achievements and success enjoyed by a younger relation. If he is able to invest any spare money, he could find that a long-term investment or savings policy will prove a useful asset in years to come.

This can be an important and constructive year for the **Wood Rabbit**. However, to achieve the best results and to make the most of his many abilities, he must have some idea of what he wants to achieve in this and the next few years. Early in the year he should set himself some objectives to aim for – without this, he could all too easily drift through parts of the year and miss opportunities that would be ideally suitable for him. He should also discuss his plans and ideas with those around him and listen to those who can help him. By being determined and being sure in his mind what it is he wants to achieve, his efforts will be rewarded. The Wood Rabbit will also experience several changes over the year – either by taking a new job, by moving, by getting married or seeing an addition to his family. Any changes that occur could put pressure on the Wood Rabbit and if he feels that he needs assistance or support, he should not hesitate to ask. Those around him want his happiness and to see him succeed, and he will be greatly helped by the encouragement and support they are able to give. To shoulder too many worries or pressures all by himself is unnecessary, particularly when he has so many who can help him. Socially and domestically, this will be a happy and memorable year for him and for those Wood Rabbits who are unattached, the year is well aspected for romance and for making new friends. This will also be a reasonably good year financially for the Wood Rabbit, although he would do well to keep a watchful eye over his spending. He can at times be a little too extravagant or generous for his own good, and if he is not careful he could find that his outgoings are considerably larger than he thought!

This will be a generally good year for the **Fire Rabbit**. He will get much pleasure from his family and friends over the year and both his domestic and social life will be enjoyable. Indeed he will be very much in demand with others in 1994 and socially this will be a busy and active year for him. If he has been lonely in recent years or has had some personal problems to overcome he would do well to view this as a year of new opportunities. He should make every effort to go out more, especially to events where he can meet others. All Fire Rabbits will find that their circle of friends will increase over the year. This is also a favourable year for taking up new interests and pursuits – academic matters and cultural pursuits are particularly well aspected. The Fire Rabbit will be generally fortunate in financial matters, although if he intends to make any large purchase or involves himself in any major transaction, he would do well not to be rushed into making a decision. By looking at various options and comparing prices he could save himself a considerable amount of money. Any problems that he faces over the year are more likely to be nigglesome than serious and should he find himself in a disagreement or awkward situation, he should look for ways to compromise or try to solve the problem as quickly as he can. To become unduly anxious over any problem or allow it to linger in the background could mar what will be a generally favourable year for the Fire Rabbit. If he is able to take some breaks or short holidays over the year he will find these most beneficial for him. This is also an ideal year for visiting friends or relations he has not seen for some time or for renewing old friendships.

This can be a very positive year for the **Earth Rabbit**. However, to do well he needs to persevere in his various activities and not allow any set-backs or problems to weaken his resolve. By being determined, giving himself priorities and following up any opportunities that he sees, the Earth Rabbit can make good progress. Business and work matters are well aspected and many Earth Rabbits will obtain a new job or be given increased responsibilities as the year progresses. The Earth Rabbit will also see an improvement in his financial situation over the year, although it would be in his interests to keep a close watch over his level of expenditure. Any savings that he can make can usefully be put towards holidays and any home improvements he wishes to carry out. The Earth Rabbit will lead a pleasant domestic and social life, and his family and friends will be most supportive to him over the year. If he needs advice and assistance with any of his enterprises he will find this readily forthcoming. Also, many Earth Rabbits can look forward to being involved in a family celebration over the year and the Earth Rabbit himself could have good cause to celebrate the realization of an ambition or the successful completion of a project with which he has been involved. He will also derive much satisfaction from his hobbies and interests in 1994, especially if they involve him in creative or outdoor activities.

Famous Rabbits

Prince Albert, Cecil Beaton, Harry Belafonte, Ingrid Bergman, Melvyn Bragg, Gordon Brown, Lewis Carroll, Fidel Castro, John Cleese, Confucius, Marie Curie, Kenny Dalglish, Peter Davison, Ken Dodd, Paul Eddington, Albert Einstein, Peter Falk, W.C. Fields, James Fox, David Frost, James Galway, Cary Grant, John Gummer, Sir Richard Hadlee, Oliver Hardy, Bob Hope, Whitney Houston, John Hurt, Clive James, David Jason, Anatoli Karpov, Gary Kasparov, Penelope Keith, Cheryl Ladd, Julian Lennon, Patrick Lichfield, Ali MacGraw, George Michael, Roger Moore, Malcolm Muggeridge, Brian Mulroney, Nanette Newman, Christina Onassis, George Orwell, John Peel, Eva Peron, Edith Piaf, Denis Quilley, John Ruskin, Ken Russell, Mort Sahl, Elisabeth Schwarzkopf, George C. Scott, Selina Scott, Terry Scott, Sir Walter Scott, Neil Sedaka, Gillian Shephard, Georges Simenon, Neil Simon, Frank Sinatra, Dusty Springfield, Sting, Jimmy Tarbuck, Sir Denis Thatcher, J.R.R. Tolkien, Arturo Toscanini, Tina Turner, Luther Vandross, Queen Victoria, Terry Waite, Andy Warhol, Orson Welles.

The Dragon

16 February 1904	to 3 February 1905	***Wood Dragon***
3 February 1916	to 22 January 1917	***Fire Dragon***
23 January 1928	to 9 February 1929	***Earth Dragon***
8 February 1940	to 26 January 1941	***Metal Dragon***
27 January 1952	to 13 February 1953	***Water Dragon***
13 February 1964	to 1 February 1965	***Wood Dragon***
31 January 1976	to 17 February 1977	***Fire Dragon***
17 February 1988	to 5 February 1989	***Earth Dragon***

The Personality of the Dragon

Know what you want to do, hold the thought firmly, and do every day what should be done, and every sunset will see you that much nearer the goal.

– Elbert Hubbard: a Dragon.

The Dragon is born under the sign of luck. He is a proud and lively character and has a tremendous amount of self-confidence. He is also highly intelligent and very quick to take advantage of any opportunities that occur. He is ambitious and determined and will do well in practically anything which he attempts. He is also something of a perfectionist and will always try and maintain the high standards which he sets himself.

The Dragon does not suffer fools gladly and will be quick to criticize anyone or anything that displeases him. He can be blunt and forthright in his views and is certainly not renowned for being either tactful or diplomatic. He does, however, often take people at their word and can occasionally be rather gullible. If he ever feels that his trust has been abused or his dignity wounded he can sometimes become very bitter and it will take him a long time to forgive and forget.

The Dragon is usually very outgoing and is particularly adept at attracting attention and publicity. He enjoys being in the limelight and is often at his best when he is confronted by a difficult problem or tense situation. In some respects he is a showman and he rarely lacks an audience. His views and opinions are very highly valued and he invariably has something interesting – and sometimes controversial – to say.

He has considerable energy and is often prepared to work long and unsocial hours in order to achieve what he wants. He can, however, be rather impulsive and does not always consider the consequences of his actions. He also has a tendency to live for the moment and there is nothing that riles him more than to be kept waiting. The Dragon hates delay and can get extremely impatient and irritable over even the smallest of hold-ups.

The Dragon has an enormous faith in his abilities, but he does run the risk of becoming over-confident and unless he is careful he can sometimes make grave errors of judgement. While this may prove disastrous at the time, he does have the tenacity and ability to bounce back and pick up the pieces again.

The Dragon has such an assertive personality, so much will-power and such a desire to succeed that he will often reach the top of his chosen profession. He has considerable leadership qualities and will do well in positions where he can put his own ideas and policies into practice. He is usually successful in politics, show business, as the manager of his own department or business, and in any job which brings him into contact with the media.

The Dragon relies a tremendous amount on his own

judgement and can be scornful of other people's advice. He likes to feel self-sufficient, and there are many Dragons who cherish their independence to such a degree that they prefer to remain single throughout their lives. However, the Dragon will often have numerous admirers and there are many who are attracted by his flamboyant personality and striking looks. If he does marry, he will usually marry young and will find himself particularly well-suited to those born under the signs of the Snake, Rat, Monkey and Rooster. He will also find the Rabbit, Pig, Horse and Goat make ideal companions and will readily join in with many of his escapades. Two Dragons will also get on well together as they understand each other, but the Dragon may not find things so easy with the Ox and Dog as both will be critical of his impulsive and somewhat extrovert manner. He will also find it difficult to form an alliance with the Tiger, for the Tiger, like the Dragon, tends to speak his mind, is very strong-willed and likes to take the lead.

The female Dragon knows what she wants in life and sets about everything she does in a very determined and positive manner. No job is too small for her and she is often prepared to work extremely hard until she has secured her objective. She is immensely practical and somewhat liberated. She hates being bound by routine and petty restrictions and likes to have sufficient freedom to be able to go off and do what she wants to do. She will keep her house tidy but is not one for spending hours on housework – there are far too many other things that she feels are more important and that she prefers to do. Like her male counterpart, she has a tendency to speak her mind.

The Dragon usually has many interests and enjoys sport and other outdoor activities. He also likes to travel and often prefers to visit places that are off the beaten track rather than head for popular tourist attractions. He has a very adventurous streak in him and providing his financial circumstances permit – and the Dragon is usually sensible with his money – he will travel considerable distances during his lifetime.

The Dragon is a very flamboyant character and while he can be demanding of others and in his early years rather precocious, he will have many friends and will nearly always be the centre of attention. He has charisma and so much confidence in himself that he can often become a source of inspiration for others. In China he is the leader of the carnival and he is also blessed with an inordinate share of luck.

The Five Different Types of Dragon

In addition to the 12 signs of the Chinese zodiac, there are five elements and these have a strengthening or moderating influence on the sign. The effects of the five elements on the Dragon are described below, together with the years in which the elements were exercising their influence. Therefore all Dragons born in 1940 are Metal Dragons, those born in 1952 are Water Dragons, and so on.

Metal Dragon: 1940
This Dragon is very strong-willed and has a particularly forceful personality. He is energetic, ambitious and tries to be scrupulous in his dealings with others. He can also be blunt and to the point and usually has no hesitation in speaking his mind. If people disagree with him, or are not prepared to co-operate, he is more than happy to go his own way. The Metal Dragon usually has very high moral values and is held in great esteem by his friends and colleagues.

Water Dragon: 1952
This Dragon is friendly, easy-going and intelligent. He is quick-witted and rarely lets an opportunity slip by. However, he is not as impatient as some of the other types of Dragon and is more prepared to wait for results rather

than expect everything to happen that moment. He has an understanding nature and is prepared to share his ideas and co-operate with others. His main failing, though, is a tendency to jump from one thing to another rather than concentrate on the job in hand. He has a good sense of humour and is an effective speaker.

Wood Dragon: 1904, 1964
The Wood Dragon is practical, imaginative and inquisitive. He loves delving into all manner of subjects and can quite often come up with some highly original ideas. He is a thinker and a doer and has sufficient drive and commitment to put many of his ideas into practice. He is more diplomatic than some of the other types of Dragon and has a good sense of humour. He is very astute in business matters and can also be most generous.

Fire Dragon: 1916, 1976
This Dragon is ambitious, articulate and has a tremendous desire to succeed. He is a hard and conscientious worker and is often admired for his integrity and forthright nature. He is very strong-willed and has considerable leadership qualities. He can, however, rely a bit too much on his own judgement and fail to take into account the views and feelings of others. He can also be rather aloof and it would certainly be in his own interests to let others join in more with his various activities. The Fire Dragon usually gets much enjoyment from music, literature and the arts.

Earth Dragon: 1928, 1988
The Earth Dragon tends to be quieter and more reflective than some of the other types of Dragon. He has a wide variety of interests and is keenly aware of what is going on around him. He also has clear objectives and usually has no problems in obtaining support and backing for any of his ventures. He is very astute in financial matters and is often able to accumulate considerable wealth. He is a good

organizer, although he can at times be rather bureaucratic and fussy. He mixes well with others and has a large circle of friends.

Prospects for the Dragon in 1994

The Chinese New Year starts on 10 February 1994. Until then, the old year, the Year of the Rooster, is still making its presence felt.

The Year of the Rooster (23 January 1993 to 9 February 1994) will have been a generally good year for the Dragon and in what remains of the year, he should make the most of the favourable trends that prevail. He should pursue any opportunities that he sees and make every attempt to advance his ideas and plans. His achievements in the latter part of the Rooster year can be quite considerable, but to achieve success he needs to be bold, assertive and determined.

At this time the Dragon will find that those around him are supportive and will give him valuable help and advice with his various activities. He will, in any case, be much in demand with his family and friends. For those who are unattached, the prospects for making new friends and for romance are particularly encouraging in the second half of the Rooster year.

The Rooster year will, however, have been quite a demanding year for the Dragon and he would do well to make sure that he allows himself the opportunity to unwind and to have a break from his usual everyday activities. If he sets a regular time aside for his hobbies and recreational pursuits, he will feel considerably revitalized.

Many Dragons will travel considerable distances in the latter part of the Rooster year and to ensure his journeys work out well, the Dragon should make sure that all his travel documentation is in order and that he has checked any connections he has to make. To leave travel arrangements to the last moment could cause problems and mar what will otherwise be a good time away.

The Dragon will have several strokes of luck towards the end of the Rooster year and it could be in his interests to enter any competitions that catch his eye.

The Year of the Dog starts on 10 February 1994 and will be a mixed year for the Dragon. He may find that he is not able to accomplish as much as he would like over the year and that some of his plans may be subject to delay and alteration. While this may make disappointing reading for the Dragon, the year need not be a bad one. Much depends on his attitude and his willingness to co-operate with others. Providing he is careful and cautious, the Dog year can prove quite a satisfying and rewarding time for him. However, if the Dragon decides to retain an independent stance and acts impulsively and without thinking through the consequences of his actions, problems and disappointments will arise. This is a year for moderation, caution and careful planning.

There are several areas in particular in which the Dragon needs to exercise care. One of these areas is finance: the Dragon should be very careful when dealing with monetary matters. He would do well to keep a close watch on his outgoings and make sure that he understands all the implications of any large financial agreement or transaction that he enters. Providing he is cautious and prudent all will be well, but this is not a year when he can afford to take risks with his money.

Another area which could cause problems is his relations with others. In 1994 the Dragon should be tactful and diplomatic. Sometimes he can be rather forthright in expressing his views and, if he is not careful, he could strain his normally good relations with those around him as well as reducing the level of support that he might otherwise obtain. Throughout the Dog year, the Dragon does need to pay close attention to the views and feelings of those around him and, as far as possible, steer clear of arguments or confrontations. To upset others could rebound on him and this is something he should try to avoid.

However, while his relations with others do need careful handling, socially this will still be an active year for him. Many Dragons will find that their circle of friends and acquaintances will increase quite substantially over the year and the Dragon can look forward to attending several memorable and enjoyable social functions. For those Dragons who are unattached, there will be some excellent opportunities to meet others and build up new friendships.

The Dragon can also look forward to making steady progress in his work. He should promote any ideas that he has and his resourcefulness and quick-thinking will be very much appreciated by those around him. He should also pursue any opportunities for advancement that he sees. Those Dragons seeking work should remain persistent and follow up any opportunities that they see. It might be useful for them to look at types of work which they might not have fully considered before and, if possible, try to add to their skills and qualifications over the year. Any additional experience or knowledge they can gain will do much to enhance their prospects both in this and future years.

The Dragon will lead a pleasant domestic life in 1994. However, he would do well to involve others in his activities and also, if he does have any matters that are causing him concern, to seek the advice of those around him. To keep any problems or worries to himself will only add to his own burden and possibly make him more tense and irritable. His family and friends are there to help and advise him and the Dragon would be greatly helped by confiding in others.

The Dragon will derive much pleasure from his hobbies and interests over the year and, even though he may be very busy at times, it is important that he allows himself time for recreational pursuits. Although he is usually blessed with considerable stamina, to drive himself relentlessly and not give himself the chance to relax and restore lost energy could leave him feeling listless and prone to colds and other minor ailments. If he does not get much exercise during the day, the Dragon will find that some additional and suitable exercise will do much to improve his well-being.

There will be several opportunities for the Dragon to travel in 1994 and his travel plans and any holidays he takes will go well. Travel will prove most beneficial for him.

Although 1994 will not be without its difficulties, the year need not be an adverse one. Providing the Dragon is careful in monetary matters, handles his relations with others with care and continues to set about his activities in his usual resourceful way, he will do well. As far as possible he should avoid taking risks and keep a close watch over his rather impulsive nature.

The Dragon will, however, find that the year will improve as it goes on and from October onwards he will begin to see a noticeable upturn in his fortunes, an upturn which will continue in 1995. It will also be in the latter part of the year that the Dragon will be able to make the best progress.

As far as the different types of Dragon are concerned, 1994 could be a tricky year for the **Metal Dragon**. Despite his many capabilities and qualities, the Metal Dragon can be forthright in his views and likes to retain a certain amount of independence in his actions. Both these traits could cause him problems in 1994. To achieve the best results over the year the Metal Dragon needs to be patient, diplomatic and willing to involve others in his activities. He also needs to show a certain amount of flexibility in any awkward situations in which he finds himself. If he can do this – and it may not always be easy – he will find life much easier and his progress that much more satisfying. To ignore the views and opinions of others and to adopt a go-it-alone attitude could leave him isolated and lacking support when he needs it. However, despite the variable aspects that exist, this need not be too bad a year and indeed 1994 will hold some very enjoyable and satisfying times for the Metal Dragon. With determination and commitment he can do well in his work and many Metal Dragons will, towards the end of the year, take on new and more interesting responsibilities. The Metal Dragon will also lead an active social life and be invited to several most enjoyable functions. His domestic life will also be content, although to preserve domestic harmony he does need to take into account the views of those around him and not become so preoccupied with his own concerns that he ignores the interests of others. Travel is well aspected and in view of the generally demanding nature of the year, the Metal Dragon would do well to ensure that he gets away for at least one good break in 1994.

This will be an important year for the **Water Dragon**, and for those Water Dragons who have been experiencing problems and uncertainties, the year can bring new and brighter prospects. The Water Dragon can regard 1994 as a year of hope and over the course of it he will begin to see some positive changes taking place. In the early stages of the year he would do well to consider his present position and what it is that he would like to achieve in the near future. Then, with some plan or idea in mind, he should set about achieving his objective. With his usual determined spirit and persuasive personality, the Water Dragon can achieve much in the year and build a good foundation on which to expand in the future. He should pursue any opportunities that he sees, particularly in his work, and if he is able to add to his skills he will find that this will prove an excellent asset in future years. Work and career prospects will generally go well in 1994. The Water Dragon will, however, need to watch his finances carefully – this will be quite an expensive year for him and he may have to exercise restraint in his spending. Like all Dragons, the Water Dragon cannot take unnecessary risks over the year and while the aspects – certainly as far as his work is concerned – are generally favourable, he does need to plan carefully and to avoid making hurried or rash decisions. The Water Dragon will obtain considerable pleasure from the achievements of a younger relation over the year, although he may also have to assist another relative who has some difficulty to overcome. Any help and assistance he can give will be very much appreciated. This will be a good year for travel.

This will be a variable year for the **Wood Dragon**. Changes could take place in almost any aspect of his life – his personal circumstances, career or accommodation. In this respect the year will contain moments of uncertainty and anxiety. However, the Wood Dragon should not get disheartened by this. The changes that occur will work out positively for him and even though he may have to rethink some of his plans and objectives, new and interesting opportunities will almost certainly arise. In many ways 1994 will herald a new and positive chapter of his life and the events that occur and the action that he takes will prove of considerable significance to him in the future. The Wood Dragon will also be greatly assisted by those around him and he would do well to seek the opinion and advice of others on any matter that might be troubling him. In view of the many demands and pressures that he will face over the year, it is essential that he allows himself the opportunity to relax and sets some time aside for recreational pursuits. The Wood Dragon will travel considerable distances over the year and he is likely to find the journeys and holidays that he undertakes particularly pleasurable. He does, however, need to keep a watch on his level of spending over the year and also on any new financial commitments that he takes on. To stretch his resources too far could cause problems. The Wood Dragon will see a noticeable upturn in his fortunes from the late summer onwards.

The **Fire Dragon** has many talents and admirable qualities, but unfortunately one which he sometimes lacks is patience and in 1994 patience is a quality which he will need! Although he can look forward to making a certain amount of progress over the year, he cannot be overambitious in his activities. He could find some of his plans subject to delay or alteration. However, if he is prepared to be patient and adaptable, he will find that the events of the year will, in the end, work out very much in his favour. He will also fare much better if he concentrates on certain objectives rather than spreading his energies out too widely. His work will bring new and interesting opportunities and all Fire Dragons would do well to try and add to their skills and qualifications over the year. The skills that the Fire Dragon learns and the experience he gains will prove of considerable value to him in the future. He will lead an enjoyable social life over the year and many Fire Dragons will make new friends and could meet their future partner in the year. Socially, this will be a happy year for the Fire Dragon, although there is still a possibility that he could find himself involved in a difference of opinion with someone. If such a situation arises, he would do well to sort the matter out as quickly and as amicably as he can. He should also listen to and bear in mind the viewpoints of others – particularly if they speak with experience. To be intransigent and inflexible in an awkward situation could only make matters worse and sour what will generally be a good year for him. While the year is not a bad one financially, the summer months could prove quite expensive for the Fire Dragon and it would be in his interest to keep a close watch on his level of expenditure at this time.

This will be reasonably good year for the **Earth Dragon**. He will obtain considerable pleasure from any travelling that he undertakes and from his hobbies and interests. Socially, this will also be a most pleasant year and the Earth Dragon can look forward to having some enjoyable times with his family and friends. However, while the year will contain many pleasurable moments, the Earth Dragon may still have a few problems to contend with. He needs to deal with important forms and items of correspondence with care and, while he is usually most particular when dealing with financial matters, he should not enter into any large transaction or new financial commitment unless he has studied all the facts and implications beforehand. If in doubt over any matter, he would do well to seek the advice of those he can trust. The Earth Dragon also needs to be careful when handling any potentially dangerous pieces of equipment or when moving heavy objects. By ignoring precautions he could accidentally strain or injure himself and would do well to remember the old saying 'It is better to be safe than sorry.' Generally, however, the year will hold some happy times for the Earth Dragon and in addition to being in demand with his family and friends, he will make satisfying progress in his various interests and activities.

Famous Dragons

Jenny Agutter, Moira Anderson, Jeffrey Archer, Joan Baez, Peter Barkworth, Roseanne Barr, Count Basie, Simon Bates, Stanley Baxter, Saint Bernadette, Geoff Boycott, Tim Brooke-Taylor, Sir Alastair Burnet, Jennifer Capriati, Neneh Cherry, Julie Christie, Kenneth Clarke, James Coburn, Bing Crosby, Roald Dahl, Salvador Dali, Robert De Niro, Susan Dey, Neil Diamond, Matt Dillon, Placido Domingo, Val Doonican, Faye Dunaway, Prince Edward, Roberta Flack, Bruce Forsyth, Michael Gambon, Sir John Gielgud, Graham Greene, Che Guevara, Edward Heath, James Herriot, Gloria Hunniford, Joan of Arc, Tom Jones, Martin Luther King, Ian Lang, Bonnie Langford, John Lennon, Abraham Lincoln, Gina Lollobrigida, Queen Margrethe II of Denmark, Yehudi Menuhin, François Mitterrand, Bob Monkhouse, Desmond Morris, Johnny Morris, Hosni Mubarak, Florence Nightingale, Elaine Paige, Gregory Peck, Richard Pryor, Esther Rantzen, Christopher Reeve, Cliff Richard, George Bernard Shaw, Eduard Shevardnadze, Mel Smith, Ringo

Starr, Princess Stephanie of Monaco, Karlheinz Stockhausen, Shirley Temple, Christopher Timothy, Raquel Welch, Mae West, Lord Wilson of Rievaulx (Harold Wilson), Susannah York, Frank Zappa.

The Snake

4 February 1905 to	24 January 1906	*Wood Snake*
23 January 1917 to	10 February 1918	*Fire Snake*
10 February 1929 to	29 January 1930	*Earth Snake*
27 January 1941 to	14 February 1942	*Metal Snake*
14 February 1953 to	2 February 1954	*Water Snake*
2 February 1965 to	20 January 1966	*Wood Snake*
18 February 1977 to	6 February 1978	*Fire Snake*
6 February 1989 to	26 January 1990	*Earth Snake*

The Personality of the Snake

The greatest thing in this world is not so much where we are, but in what direction we are moving.
– *Oliver Wendell Holmes: a Snake.*

The Snake is born under the sign of wisdom. He is highly intelligent and his mind is forever active. He is always planning and always looking for ways in which he can use his considerable skills. He is a deep thinker and likes to meditate and reflect.

Many times during his life he will shed one of his famous Snake skins and take up new interests or start a completely different job. The Snake enjoys a challenge and he rarely makes mistakes. He is a skilful organizer, has considerable business acumen and is usually lucky in money matters. Most Snakes are financially secure in their later years provided they do not gamble – the Snake has the distinction of being the worst gambler in the whole of the Chinese zodiac!

The Snake generally has a calm and placid nature and prefers the quieter things in life. He does not like to be in a frenzied atmosphere and hates being hurried into making a quick decision. He also does not like interference in his affairs and tends to rely on his own judgement rather than listen to advice.

The Snake can at times appear solitary. He is quiet, reserved and sometimes has difficulty in communicating with others. He has little time for idle gossip and will certainly not suffer fools gladly. He does, however, have a good sense of humour, and this is particularly appreciated in times of crisis.

The Snake is certainly not afraid of hard work and is thorough in all that he does. He is very determined and can occasionally be ruthless in order to achieve his aims. His confidence, will-power and quick thinking usually ensure his success, but should he fail it will often take a long time for him to recover. He cannot bear failure and is a very bad loser.

The Snake can also be evasive and does not willingly let people into his confidence. This secrecy and distrust can sometimes work against him and it is a trait which all Snakes should try to overcome.

Another characteristic of the Snake is his tendency to rest after any sudden or prolonged bout of activity. He burns up so much nervous energy that without proper care he can – if he is not careful – be susceptible to high blood pressure and nervous disorders.

It has sometimes been said that the Snake is a late starter in life and this is mainly because it often takes him a while to find a job with which he is genuinely happy. However, the Snake will usually do well in any position which involves research and writing and where he is given sufficient freedom to develop his own ideas and plans. He makes a good teacher, politician, personnel manager and social adviser.

The Snake chooses his friends carefully and, while he

keeps a tight control over his finances, he can be particularly generous to those he likes. He will think nothing of buying expensive gifts or treating his friends or loved ones to the best theatre seats in town. In return he demands loyalty. The Snake is very possessive and he can become extremely jealous and hurt if he finds his trust has been abused.

The Snake is also renowned for his good looks and is never short of admirers. The female Snake in particular is most alluring. She has style, grace and excellent (and usually expensive) taste in clothes. A keen socializer, she is likely to have a wide range of friends and has a happy knack of impressing those who matter. She has numerous interests and her advice and opinions are often highly valued. She is generally a calm-natured person and while she involves herself in many activities, she likes to retain a certain amount of privacy in the things that she does.

The affairs of the heart are very important to the Snake and he will often have many romances before he finally settles down. He will find that he is particularly well suited to those born under the signs of the Ox, Dragon, Rabbit and Rooster. Provided the Snake is allowed sufficient freedom to pursue his own interests, he can also build up a very satisfactory relationship with the Rat, Horse, Goat, Monkey and Dog, but he should try to steer clear of another Snake as they could very easily become jealous of each other. The Snake will also have difficulty in getting on with the honest and down-to-earth Pig, and will find the Tiger far too much of a disruptive influence on his quiet and peace-loving ways.

The Snake certainly appreciates the finer things in life. He enjoys good food and often takes a keen interest in the arts. He also enjoys reading and is invariably drawn to subjects such as philosophy, political thought, religion or the occult. He is fascinated by the unknown and his enquiring mind is always looking for answers. Some of the world's most original thinkers have been Snakes, and –

although he may not readily admit it – the Snake is often psychic and relies a lot on intuition.

The Snake is certainly not the most energetic member of the Chinese zodiac. He prefers to proceed at his own pace and to do the things he wants. He is very much his own master and throughout his life he will try his hand at many things. The Snake is something of a dabbler, but at some time – and usually when he least expects it – his hard work and his efforts will be recognized and he will invariably meet with the success and the financial security which he so much desires.

The Five Different Types of Snake

In addition to the 12 signs of the Chinese zodiac, there are five elements and these have a strengthening or moderating influence on the sign. The effects of the five elements on the Snake are described below, together with the years in which the elements were exercising their influence. Therefore all Snakes born in 1941 are Metal Snakes, those born in 1893 and 1953 are Water Snakes, and so on.

Metal Snake: 1941
This Snake is quiet, confident and fiercely independent. He often prefers to work on his own and will only let a privileged few into his confidence. He is quick to spot opportunities and will set about achieving his objectives with an awesome determination. He is astute in financial matters and will often invest his money well. He also has a liking for the finer things in life and has a good appreciation of the arts, literature, music and good food. He usually has a small group of extremely good friends and can be generous to his loved ones.

Water Snake: 1893, 1953
This Snake has a wide variety of interests. He enjoys

studying all manner of subjects and is capable of undertaking quite detailed research and becoming a specialist in his chosen area. He is highly intelligent, has a good memory, and is particularly astute when dealing with business and financial matters. He tends to be quietly spoken and a little reserved, but he does have sufficient strength of character to make his views known and attain his ambitions. He is very loyal to his family and friends.

Wood Snake: 1905, 1965
The Wood Snake has a friendly temperament and a good understanding of human nature. He is able to communicate well with others and often has many friends and admirers. He is witty, intelligent and ambitious. He has numerous interests and prefers to live in a quiet, stable environment where he can work without too much interference. He enjoys the arts and usually derives much pleasure from collecting paintings and antiques. His advice is often very highly valued, particularly on social and domestic matters.

Fire Snake: 1917, 1977
The Fire Snake tends to be more forceful, outgoing and energetic than some of the other types of Snake. He is ambitious, confident and never slow in voicing his opinions – and he can be very abrasive to those he does not like. He does, however, have many leadership qualities and can win the respect and support of many with his firm and resolute manner. He usually has a good sense of humour, a wide circle of friends and a very active social life. The Fire Snake is also a keen traveller.

Earth Snake: 1929, 1989
The Earth Snake is charming, amusing and has a very amiable manner. He is conscientious and reliable in his work and approaches everything he does in a level-headed and sensible way. He can, however, tend to err on the cautious side and never likes to be hassled into making a

decision. He is extremely adept in dealing with financial matters and is a shrewd investor. He has many friends and is very supportive towards the members of his family.

Prospects for the Snake in 1994

The Chinese New Year starts on 10 February 1994. Until then, the old year, the Year of the Rooster, is still making its presence felt.

The Year of the Rooster (23 January 1993 to 9 February 1994) will have been a very positive year for the Snake and for what remains of the year the Snake should make the most of the favourable trends that exist. He should pursue his aims and aspirations, and if he sees the chance of seizing an opportunity which he feels would be to his advantage, the Snake should act. He can accomplish much at this time and, by being alert to all that is going on around him, can make excellent progress.

The aspects are most favourable for his career at this time and Snakes seeking employment or looking for a change in their work should follow up any vacancies that attract their attention. The Snake could also find that a skill of his proves particularly useful and any Snake interested in the performing arts or with some creative talent should promote or further his interests. In the closing stages of the Rooster year, fortune favours the bold Snake.

The Snake can also look forward to having some most pleasant times with his family and friends and a new acquaintance that he makes in the closing months of the year will be of considerable importance to him in the future.

The one area where the Snake should exercise caution is with finance. Although he is usually most careful in financial matters, he does need to keep a watchful eye over his general level of expenditure in the closing stages of the Rooster year. He should also be wary of getting involved in any risky or speculative ventures at this time because he could, without care, end up the loser.

Generally, however, by pursuing his aims and objectives, the Snake will do well at the end of the Rooster year and this positive trend will, for the most part, continue into the next Chinese year.

The Year of the Dog begins on 10 February 1994 and will be a pleasing year for the Snake. He will be able to make considerable progress in many of his activities, although this will not be possible without much effort on his part.

For all their commendable qualities, some Snakes do have a lazy streak in them and it is this streak they will need to watch over the year. If the Snake is just prepared to rest on past achievements and not exert himself, this will lead to problems and disappointments. But if he remains committed to his aims and gives of his best, then he will enjoy considerable success and reap the rewards of his efforts.

In his work, there will be plenty of opportunities for the Snake to demonstrate his talents. He should advance any new ideas that he has and pursue any opportunities that he sees. This is a good year for starting new projects or widening experience by branching out into new areas. Admittedly, not all that the Snake attempts will work out as he intends and he may have to modify some of his ideas, but providing he is prepared to be flexible in his outlook and not be deterred by minor set-backs, this will be a positive and rewarding year for him. Those Snakes who are seeking work should again pursue any openings that they see but also approach those who may be in a position to help them. By taking the initiative and taking positive action, the Snake will achieve some very worthwhile and constructive results in 1994. Indeed, throughout the year he would do well to remember the saying 'Nothing ventured, nothing gained.'

The Snake will also be fortunate in financial matters and most Snakes will end the year in a much healthier financial position than at the start. However, the Snake cannot afford to be complacent in financial matters and would do well to avoid any risky undertakings or gambling with his money. Snakes are not usually lucky when they gamble and it is a warning the Snake would do well to remember throughout the year. Provided he is cautious and careful, financial matters will go well.

The Snake's family will be most important to him over the year and will give him encouragement in any venture with which he is involved. Although there are some Snakes who prefer to retain a certain independence, even secrecy, in their actions, it would be in their interests to open up and be more forthcoming. By involving others in his plans and activities and seeking their opinions, the Snake will receive much useful advice and support.

The Snake will lead a quiet but pleasant social life over the year. For any Snake who may have felt lonely in recent times, there will be opportunities to make new friends but, as with most things in 1994, the Snake does need to take the initiative. To make new friends he needs to go out more, join local clubs, and be prepared to make the effort. If he does, this can be an enjoyable and happy year for him and many Snakes can look forward to establishing several new and rewarding friendships over the year.

Another area which is well aspected is travel. Many Snakes will travel considerable distances in 1994 and for those Snakes who have been thinking of broadening their experience by working in another country or undertaking a lot of travelling, this would be an ideal year to do so.

Naturally no year is without its problems and there are certain areas that the Snake would do well to watch. During the year he needs to safeguard his property and personal possessions well. Without care, he might suffer a loss or mislay something which he values – a loss which, had he taken better precautions, could have been averted. It is a warning all Snakes would do well to heed!

The second area concerns himself. Although most Snakes

will enjoy good health over the year, the Snake cannot take liberties by driving himself too hard without proper rest or, if he leads a busy life-style, by continually rushing his meals or being reliant on convenience foods. If he does, he could find himself prone to minor ailments and in 1994 he should resolve to take good care of himself, eat a healthy and well-balanced diet and exercise well. He will also find it beneficial to regularly set some time aside for recreational pursuits and do something unrelated to his usual daytime activities. A new hobby or interest could be just the tonic that he needs.

This can be a positive and constructive year for the Snake and he can realize worthy accomplishments in almost any area he chooses. However, to achieve these positive results, the Snake does need to remain committed to his aims and not be deflected by any temporary set-backs that might occur. In 1994 the amount that the Snake achieves is very much dependent on his own attitude and persistence. If he is prepared to make the effort the year will prove both rewarding and fulfilling for him.

As far as the different types of Snake are concerned, 1994 will be an important year for the **Metal Snake**. For many Metal Snakes, this will be a year in which they shed one of their Snake skins and begin a new and positive phase of life – either by moving, taking up new interests or accepting a new job. No matter what changes take place, the Metal Snake will find that they will prove invigorating and will open up new opportunities and friendships for him. Many Metal Snakes will be successful in gaining a new and more responsible position in their work over the year and the Metal Snake should remain particularly alert for positions to pursue in the early months of the Dog year and also in October and November. He could also find a special interest that he has will prove a useful asset to him and would do well to promote his talents and skills as much as he can. Travel is well aspected throughout the year and if the Metal Snake has any friends or relations that he would like to see who live a long way away, this could prove an ideal year to visit them. Although the Metal Snake usually keeps himself in trim, he will find that if does not get much exercise during the day, some suitable activity such as additional walking, swimming or a keep-fit course will do much to improve his well-being.

This will be a satisfying year for the **Water Snake**. By continuing to set about his various activities in his usual diligent and conscientious manner, he will make good progress, impress others and could be given some additional responsibilities in his work. The Water Snake should pursue any opportunities that he sees and even if he meets with the occasional set-back or reversal, he should not let this get the better of him. For the Water Snake who keeps his eyes firmly set on his goals and objectives, this can be a rewarding and fulfilling year. However, in all his activities, the Water Snake does need to obtain the support of others and be more forthcoming. At times he can be rather shy and reserved and it is a trait he would do well to overcome. The Water Snake also needs to keep a close check on his outgoings over the year as his general level of expenditure could be greater than he thought. Without care, this could lead to problems. The Water Snake's family will give him much pleasure and support in 1994 and he is likely to take particular delight in the success and progress enjoyed by a younger relation. Also, if he is able to take up a new interest or learn a new skill during the year he will find that this will give him many hours of pleasure as well as discovering talents that he never knew he had!

This will be a constructive and enjoyable year for the **Wood Snake**. Although not all his plans may work out as he would have liked, providing he is prepared to be flexible in his outlook and willing to adapt to new situations as they arise, he will do well. In his work there will be new challenges to meet and many Wood Snakes will be given a new position or increased responsibilities as the year progresses. Although the Wood Snake does need to work closely with others and cannot afford to adopt too independent an attitude, this should not stop him from acting on his own initiative, starting new projects or developing his own ideas. For the ambitious and creative Wood Snake, 1994 can be a significant year. He can also look forward to some splendid times with his family and friends and while his social life may at times be quiet, his interests will keep him content and occupied. The Wood Snake does, however, need to keep a close watch over his spending in 1994 and if he is involved in any expensive undertaking, he should make sure that he is aware of all the terms of the undertaking and can meet any obligations he might be placed under. Throughout the year the Wood Snake cannot be complacent either in financial matters or concerning any important forms that he has to complete. Travel is well aspected and many Wood Snakes are likely to travel considerable distances in 1994.

This will be a positive and constructive year for the **Fire Snake**. However, to achieve the most favourable results in 1994, he needs to concentrate on specific tasks and not waste his energies on trying to do too much too soon or rush projects he is already engaged on. Provided he sets himself clear objectives and sets about his activities in a methodical manner, he will do well. Any additional skills and qualifications that he can obtain will prove of considerable value to him and it would also be in his interests to give some thought to his plans for the future. In many ways, 1994 will not only be a year in which he can make positive progress but also one in which he can lay the foundations on which to build in the next few years. The Fire Snake will have some pleasing times with his family and friends over the year and while he could have a clash of opinion with someone, he will find a conciliatory attitude will do much to ease the problem. To remain intransigent or not be prepared to consider other points of view could make matters worse and mar what will otherwise be an enjoyable year for him. Also, if he does have any problems troubling him, particularly of a personal nature, he would do well to share his worries with others. He will be gratified and reassured by the support he is given and could even find that much of his worry is unfounded. The Fire Snake would also do well to watch his general level of spending over the year. There will, however, be several excellent opportunities for him to travel in 1994 and he is also likely to obtain considerable pleasure from outdoor activities over the year.

This will be a good, although challenging, year for the **Earth Snake**. Over the course of the year he is likely to give much thought to his future. Many Earth Snakes will move or consider moving, while others will be tempted to have alterations carried out on their property. In either case, the Earth Snake should not be rushed into making any sudden decision. Time is on his side and before making any changes he needs to consider all the implications and costs of any plans that he proposes to carry out. Then, once he is sure in his own mind that the action is right, he can proceed with confidence. The Earth Snake will also be helped over the year by the support and encouragement that those around him give. Generally, any uncertainties and dilemmas that the Earth Snake might face will occur in the first few months of the year and the latter part of the year will be a most favourable and pleasant time for him. The Earth Snake will also be able to devote considerable time to his hobbies and interests over the year and these are likely to give him much satisfaction and pleasure. If he does not already have an interest he can pursue in his spare time, he should make every effort to take one up. He could find an activity such as photography, painting, writing or making music especially enjoyable and a good outlet for his creative talents. He would also do well to try and go away for several short breaks over the year and if he is able to spread them out over the course of the year he will find these both enjoyable and most beneficial for him.

Famous Snakes

Muhammad Ali, Ann-Margret, Yasser Arafat, Paddy Ashdown, Ronnie Barker, Kim Basinger, Tony Blair, William Blake, Heinrich Böll, Betty Boothroyd, Brahms, Raymond Burr, Dick Cheney, Len Deighton, Fats Domino, Bob Dylan, Stefan Edberg, Elgar, Mahatma Gandhi, Greta Garbo, J. Paul Getty, W.E. Gladstone, Graham Gooch, Princess Grace of Monaco, Linda Gray, Bob Hawke, Nigel Hawthorne, Denis Healey, Audrey Hepburn, Jack Higgins, Paul Hogan, Michael Howard, Howard Hughes, Rev. Jesse Jackson, Derek Jameson, Griff Rhys Jones, Gorden Kaye, J.F. Kennedy, Carole King, James Last, Dame Vera Lynn, Linda McCartney, Craig McLachlan, Magnus Magnusson, Mao Tse-tung, Nigel Mansell, Dean Martin, Henri Matisse, Robert Mitchum, Nasser, Bob Newhart, Mike Oldfield, Aristotle Onassis, Jacqueline Onassis, Ryan O'Neal, Pablo Picasso, Mary Pickford, Edgar Allan Poe, Michael Portillo, André Previn, Brian Redhead, Jean-Paul Sartre, Franz Schubert, Brooke Shields, Nigel Short, Delia Smith, John Thaw, Dionne Warwick, Oprah Winfrey, Victoria Wood, Virginia Woolf, Mike Yarwood.

The Horse

25 January 1906 to	12 February 1907	*Fire Horse*
11 February 1918 to	31 January 1919	*Earth Horse*
30 January 1930 to	16 February 1931	*Metal Horse*
15 February 1942 to	4 February 1943	*Water Horse*
3 February 1954 to	23 January 1955	*Wood Horse*
21 January 1966 to	8 February 1967	*Fire Horse*
7 February 1978 to	27 January 1979	*Earth Horse*
27 January 1990 to	14 February 1991	*Metal Horse*

The Personality of the Horse

Your success depends on what you do yourself, with your own means.

— *P.T. Barnum: a Horse.*

The Horse is born under the signs of elegance and ardour. He has a most engaging and charming manner and is usually very popular. He loves meeting people and likes attending parties and other large social gatherings.

He is a lively character and enjoys being the centre of attention. He has considerable leadership qualities and is much admired for his honest and straightforward manner. He is an eloquent and persuasive speaker and has a great love of discussion and debate. The Horse also has a particularly agile mind and can assimilate facts remarkably quickly.

He does, however, have a fiery temper and although his

outbursts are usually short-lived, he can often say things which he will later regret. He is also not particularly good at keeping secrets.

The Horse has many interests and involves himself in a wide variety of activities. He can, however, get involved in so much that he can often waste his energies on projects which he never has time to complete. He also has a tendency to change his interests rather frequently and will often get caught up with the latest craze or 'in thing' until something better or more exciting turns up.

The Horse also likes to have a certain amount of freedom and independence in the things that he does. He hates being bound by petty rules and regulations and as far as possible he likes to feel that he is answerable to no one but himself. But despite this spirit of freedom, he still likes to have the support and encouragement of others in his various enterprises.

Due to his many talents and likeable nature, the Horse will often go far in life. He enjoys challenges and is a methodical and tireless worker. However, should things work against him and he fail in any of his enterprises, it will take a long time for him to recover and pick up the pieces again. Success to the Horse means everything. To fail is a disaster and a humiliation.

The Horse likes to have variety in his life and he will try his hand at many different things before he settles down to one particular job. Even then, he will probably remain alert to see if there are any new and better opportunities for him to take up. The Horse has a restless nature and can easily get bored. He does, however, excel in any position which allows him sufficient freedom to act on his own initiative or brings him into contact with a lot of people.

Although the Horse is not particularly bothered about accumulating great wealth, he handles his finances with care and will rarely experience any serious financial problems.

The Horse also enjoys travel and he loves visiting new

and far-away places. At some stage during his life he will be tempted to live abroad for a short period of time and due to his adaptable nature he will find that he will fit in well wherever he goes.

The Horse pays a great deal of attention to his appearance and usually likes to wear smart, colourful and rather distinctive clothes. He is very attractive to the opposite sex and will often have many romances before he settles down. He is loyal and protective to his partner, but despite his family commitments he still likes to retain a certain measure of independence and have the freedom to carry on with his own interests and hobbies. He will find that he is especially well-suited to those born under the signs of the Tiger, Goat, Rooster and Dog. The Horse can also get on well with the Rabbit, Dragon, Snake, Pig and another Horse, but he will find the Ox too serious and intolerant for his liking. The Horse will also have difficulty in getting on with the Monkey and the Rat – the Monkey is very inquisitive and the Rat seeks security – and both will resent the Horse's rather independent ways.

The female Horse is usually most attractive and has a friendly, outgoing personality. She is highly intelligent, has many interests and is alert to everything that is going on around her. She particularly enjoys outdoor pursuits and often likes to take part in sport and keep-fit activities. She also enjoys travel, literature and the arts, and is a very good conversationalist.

Although the Horse can be stubborn and rather self-centred, he does have a considerate nature and is often willing to help others. He has a good sense of humour and will usually make a favourable impression wherever he goes. Provided he can curb his slightly restless nature and keep a tight control over his temper, the Horse will go through life making friends, taking part in a multitude of different activities and generally achieving many of his objectives. His life will rarely be dull.

The Five Different Types of Horse

In addition to the 12 signs of the Chinese zodiac, there are five elements, and these have a strengthening or moderating influence on the sign. The effects of the five elements on the Horse are described below, together with the years in which the elements were exercising their influence. Therefore all Horses born in 1930 and 1990 are Metal Horses, those born in 1942 are Water Horses and so on.

Metal Horse: 1930, 1990
This Horse is bold, confident and forthright. He is ambitious and also a great innovator. He loves challenges and takes great delight in sorting out complicated problems. He likes to have a certain amount of independence in the things that he does and resents any outside interference. The Metal Horse has charm and a certain charisma, but he can also be very stubborn and rather impulsive. He usually has many friends and enjoys an active social life.

Water Horse: 1942
The Water Horse has a friendly nature, a good sense of humour, and is able to talk intelligently on a wide range of topics. He is astute in business matters and is quick to take advantage of any opportunities that arise. He does, however, have a tendency to get easily distracted and can change his interests – and indeed his mind – rather frequently, and this can often work to his detriment. He is nevertheless very talented and can often go far in life. He pays a great deal of attention to his appearance and is usually smart and well turned out. He loves to travel and also enjoys sport and other outdoor activities.

Wood Horse: 1894, 1954
The Wood Horse has a most agreeable and amiable nature. He communicates well with others and, like the Water

Horse, is able to talk intelligently on many different subjects. He is a hard and conscientious worker and is held in high esteem by his friends and colleagues. His opinions and views are often sought and, given his imaginative nature, he can quite often come up with some very original and practical ideas. He is usually widely read and likes to lead a busy social life. He can also be most generous and often holds high moral viewpoints.

Fire Horse: 1906, 1966
The element of Fire combined with the temperament of the Horse creates one of the most powerful forces in the Chinese zodiac. The Fire Horse is destined to lead an exciting and eventful life and to make his mark in his chosen profession. He has a forceful personality and his intelligence and resolute manner bring him the support and admiration of many. He loves action and excitement and his life will rarely be quiet. He can, however, be rather blunt and forthright in his views and does not take kindly to interference in his own affairs or to obeying orders. He is a flamboyant character, has a good sense of humour, and will lead a very active social life.

Earth Horse: 1918, 1978
This Horse is considerate and caring. He is more cautious than some of the other types of Horse, but he is wise, perceptive and extremely capable. Although he can be rather indecisive at times, he has considerable business acumen and is very astute in financial matters. He has a quiet, friendly nature and is well thought of by his family and friends.

Prospects for the Horse in 1994

The Chinese New Year starts on 10 February 1994. Until then, the old year, the Year of the Rooster, is still making its presence felt.

The Year of the Rooster (23 January 1993 to 9 February 1994) will have been a good although rather demanding year for the Horse. The remaining months of the year will continue to be busy and while there may be moments when the Horse will despair about all he has to do, he can be comforted in the knowledge that he is about to enter a new and positive phase of his life.

For what remains of the Rooster year, the Horse would do well to sort out his priorities and organize his work. Sometimes the Horse can be guilty of jumping from one activity to another without properly completing the job in hand. But by giving himself priorities and exercising a certain amount of self-discipline, he will be well satisfied with what he is able to accomplish at this time. Also, if he is able to attend to any outstanding matters or unanswered correspondence, he will find that he will be better placed to turn his attention to the new challenges and opportunities that the Year of the Dog will bring.

There is, however, one area that the Horse will need to watch in the remaining months of the Rooster year: he does need to handle his relations with others with care. He should be tactful and discreet and, as far as possible, avoid getting involved in arguments and contentious discussions. Some Horses can be quick-tempered and these would do well to remember the Chinese proverb 'Patience in a moment of anger will spare you a hundred days of anguish.' If the Horse bears this advice in mind, then he can look forward to having some most enjoyable times with his family and friends as well as receiving much useful support for his various activities. Travel is also well aspected and many Horses will travel considerable distances in the latter part of the Rooster year. The journeys and holidays that he takes are likely to prove both interesting and most enjoyable.

The Year of the Dog starts on 10 February 1994 and is going to be a positive and rewarding year for the Horse. He will be able to make considerable progress in many of his activities and can also look forward to leading a generally enjoyable domestic and social life.

To get the best results from the year, the Horse should have some idea of what he wants to achieve and then work purposefully towards that aim. Without any objective, he could miss several opportunities and not make the best use of his many talents. In 1994 the Horse needs to set about his activities in his usual resolute and determined manner and follow up any openings that he sees. This is a year of opportunity and action and it rests with the Horse to make the best use of the positive trends that prevail.

The Horse will particularly benefit from these aspects in his work and many Horses will be given new, more challenging and rewarding positions over the year. Throughout 1994 the Horse should remain alert for ways in which he can progress and, for the bold and determined Horse, the rewards of the Dog year can be great indeed.

It is also an excellent year for the Horse to widen his skills and anything that he can do to enhance his prospects will not only be to his advantage but will also bring him considerable satisfaction. Academic and cultural pursuits are both favourably aspected in 1994.

The Horse will do well in financial matters and many will see a noticeable improvement in their financial position over the year. Any Horse who may have been experiencing financial problems will see these eased as the year progresses. However, the Horse will find that if he periodically looks at his various outgoings and makes any adjustments he feels necessary, he will save himself a considerable amount of money – money which could be saved or put to more profitable use.

Domestically, the year will also contain many happy and memorable moments. The Horse's family will be a great source of pleasure to him and will give him much valuable support and encouragement in his various undertakings. He may, however, have to deal with a problem that a close relation faces over the year and his understanding manner will do much to help.

There will also be many Horses who will move house over the year and this is likely to work out well. A move could bring with it new opportunities and new friends, and many Horses will feel stimulated by a change in their environment.

Socially, 1994 will also be a pleasing year for the Horse and for the single Horse, there will be some excellent opportunities to meet others and to make new friends, especially over the summer months.

The Horse is likely to travel considerable distances in 1994 and it is a good year for him to visit places that he may have longed to see for some time, particularly those which may be off the usual tourist map. The Horse does have a definite spirit of adventure in him and his thirst for travel and for seeing unusual sites could be well satisfied over the year.

Those Horses who are sportingly inclined can also look forward to many satisfying moments over the year.

Although this will be a generally favourable year for the Horse, he may nevertheless have a few problems to deal with. These are not likely to be serious, although they could be made worse by the Horse's own attitude. If he should prove stubborn over a certain matter, particularly where a compromise is possible, he could easily upset the normally good relations that he enjoys with those around him. This in turn could create additional problems and also lessen the support that he would otherwise obtain. So, when faced with any awkward problems or situations, the Horse will find that if he is able to show a certain amount of flexibility – or at least be prepared to consider the viewpoints of others – the problem can be resolved more satisfactorily. Where compromise is not possible, patience and time could help.

The Horse should also resist the temptation to become too preoccupied with his own activities at the expense of the interests of others. Sometimes he can become so thoroughly absorbed in what he is doing that he can remain unaware of the views and the interests of those around him. To preserve good relations, he does need to bear this in mind throughout the year.

Generally, however, the Horse will enjoy 1994. The year will bring many new opportunities and, by setting about his activities in his usual determined manner, the Horse can make great progress. It will also be an active year for him – many Horses will move house, and travel and outdoor activities will figure prominently. Providing the Horse pays careful attention to the views and feelings of others, he can also look forward to some splendid times with his family and friends. This can be an exciting year for the Horse and a year of considerable achievement. In 1994 he should endeavour to make the most of the auspicious trends that prevail.

As far as the different types of Horse are concerned, this will be a pleasant and fulfilling year for the **Metal Horse**. Over the year he will not only obtain much pleasure from his existing interests, but will also find that it is an ideal time for him to take up a new hobby or interest. Anything that the Metal Horse can do to further his knowledge and interests, particularly in subjects that may be new to him, will give him much satisfaction and could be useful to him in the future. He can also look forward to some happy and memorable times with his family and friends, and many Metal Horses will have good reason for a personal or family celebration over the year. Any Metal Horse who may have been lonely in recent times should also make every effort to go out more and to meet others. Almost all Metal Horses will make some new and very good friends over the year and the Metal Horse's social life is well aspected. He will travel considerable distances over the year and if he is able to visit places which he has not seen before, he is likely to find them especially enjoyable. In many respects, 1994 is a year for experimenting, for trying new things and for satisfying his enquiring mind. Providing he uses his time constructively, the year will hold many pleasing moments for him. He will also be fortunate in financial matters and any Metal Horse who is artistically inclined or enjoys creative pursuits would do well to promote his work as much as he can. For the determined Metal Horse, this can be a most rewarding year.

This will be a highly favourable year for the **Water Horse** and over the course of the year he is likely to make considerable progress in many of his activities. New and exciting opportunities will emerge and if the Water Horse is seeking a new job or promotion, he would do well to pursue any openings that he sees. By remaining aware of all that is going on around him and being adaptable in his outlook, the Water Horse can do extremely well. He could also find it helpful to give some thought to his future objectives, to what he would like to achieve in the next few years. By doing this, he will find it easier to plan ahead and will also have a new challenge to aim for – a challenge which will give him an incentive to do well. The Water Horse's domestic and social life will be very pleasurable over the year and his family will be most supportive as well as being a source of pride to him. He will lead an active social life in 1994 and this in turn will bring him new friends and some useful acquaintances. There will be several opportunities for the Water Horse to travel and outdoor pursuits such as gardening, walking or engaging in sporting activity is likely to prove most enjoyable for him.

This will be a significant year for the **Wood Horse**. Over the course of the year he is likely to see several changes taking place, particularly as far as his work is concerned. However, despite any misgivings or uncertainties that he may have, these changes will bring with them some interesting opportunities. Throughout the year, the Wood Horse should keep his sights firmly set on his aims and ambitions and work purposefully towards achieving them.

Through an unexpected turn of events and new opportunities arising, the Wood Horse can make great progress over the year – far greater progress than he thought possible. This need not be restricted to his work, but could also apply to moving to a better location, having some alterations carried out on his home or realizing a cherished ambition. This is a year of great potential and a time for the Wood Horse to be bold, positive and go after what he himself wants. As the year will be quite demanding it is, however, essential that he does not neglect himself or those around him. He should set a regular time aside for his own recreational pursuits and also avoid the temptation of becoming so preoccupied with his own activities that he does not spend as much time with his family and friends as he should. Providing he remembers this, and also, as far as possible, spreads his workload out, the year will be very pleasant for him as well as successful. The Wood Horse will enjoy the travelling that he undertakes and a holiday or break taken in the latter part of the year is likely to prove especially enjoyable.

The **Fire Horse** will enjoy 1994, particularly because of the opportunities that the year will bring. He should continue to set about his various activities in his usual conscientious manner, while remaining alert for opportunities to pursue and for ways in which he can make the best use of his many talents. With his outgoing charm and his quick-thinking, the Fire Horse will impress many over the year, including those who hold influence and who can help his progress. The opportunities for advancement are certainly there and it rests with the Fire Horse to make the best use of these favourable trends. Fire Horses who are seeking work or who are not happy in their present occupation would do well to look at areas they might not have fully considered before. Change and new challenges often bring out the best in the Fire Horse and 1994 will be no exception. He will have some particularly memorable times with his family and friends over the year and many

Fire Horses will see an addition to their family. The Fire Horse does, however, need to watch his outgoings in 1994 – sometimes he can be rather extravagant in his spending and, by being careful, he could put any money he saves to more profitable use later. Generally, this will be a constructive and important year for the Fire Horse and, given his sense of adventure and strong personality, it will be a year he will greatly enjoy.

This will be an important year for the **Earth Horse**, not only for what he achieves but also for what he learns. By setting about his various activities in his usual methodical way and by pursuing specific objectives he will do well. The Earth Horse should, however, resist the temptation to undertake too many activities at the same time. In 1994 it is a case of concentrating on priorities. By doing this, the Earth Horse will make considerable progress as well as lay the foundations on which to build in the future. Academic pursuits are very well aspected and if the Earth Horse is able to add to his skills and qualifications over the year, he will find that this will prove a useful asset to him in the future. The Earth Horse will lead an active social life in 1994 and many Earth Horses will build up some new and meaningful friendships as the year progresses. While this will be a generally favourable year for the Earth Horse, he may, however, have to overcome a few problems. These could involve a difference of opinion with someone or an alteration of plans to fit in with changed circumstances. In either case, the problems will not be serious and while they may cause the Earth Horse some anxiety at the time, he would do well to view them as part of life's rich learning experience. Also, any difficulties that he has to face will help to focus his attention on his present situation and his future, and this in itself is very much in his interests. He would also be helped by discussing any concerns that he might have with others – he will be grateful for the advice he is given and throughout the year those around him will be most supportive and encouraging. The experience he gains and the undoubted progress he will make over the year will stand him in good stead for the future.

Famous Horses

Neil Armstrong, Rowan Atkinson, Cheryl Baker, James Baker, King Baudouin of Belgium, Margaret Beckett, Samuel Beckett, Leonard Bernstein, Sir John Betjeman, Karen Black, Gayle Blakeney, Gillian Blakeney, Nicholas Brady, Leonid Brezhnev, Ray Charles, Chopin, Sean Connery, Billy Connolly, Catherine Cookson, Ronnie Corbett, Elvis Costello, Kevin Costner, Jim Davidson, James Dean, Anne Diamond, Clint Eastwood, Thomas Alva Edison, Linda Evans, Chris Evert, Harrison Ford, Aretha Franklin, Sir Bob Geldof, Billy Graham, Larry Grayson, Sally Gunnell, Gene Hackman, Susan Hampshire, Rolf Harris, Rita Hayworth, Jimmy Hendrix, Ted Hughes, David Hunt, Douglas Hurd, Janet Jackson, Gerald Kaufman, Nikita Khrushchev, Robert Kilroy-Silk, Neil Kinnock, Dr Helmut Kohl, Eddie Large, Lenin, Annie Lennox, Syd Little, Desmond Lynam, Paul McCartney, Harold Macmillan, Nelson Mandela, Princess Margaret, Spike Milligan, Ben Murphy, Sir Isaac Newton, Louis Pasteur, Harold Pinter, J.B. Priestley, Puccini, Claire Rayner, Rembrandt, Ruth Rendell, Franklin D. Roosevelt, Anwar Sadat, Paul Simon, Peter Sissons, Lord Snowdon, Alexander Solzhenitsyn, Lisa Stansfield, Barbra Streisand, Patrick Swayze, John Travolta, Freddie Trueman, Kathleen Turner, Mike Tyson, Vivaldi, Lord Whitelaw, Andy Williams, the Duke of Windsor, Tammy Wynette, Boris Yeltsin, Michael York.

The Goat

13 February 1907 to	1 February 1908	*Fire Goat*
1 February 1919 to	19 February 1920	*Earth Goat*
17 February 1931 to	5 February 1932	*Metal Goat*
5 February 1943 to	24 January 1944	*Water Goat*
24 January 1955 to	11 February 1956	*Wood Goat*
9 February 1967 to	29 January 1968	*Fire Goat*
28 January 1979 to	15 February 1980	*Earth Goat*
15 February 1991 to	3 February 1992	*Metal Goat*

The Personality of the Goat

Diligence is the mother of good fortune.
– *Miguel de Cervantes: a Goat.*

The Goat is born under the sign of art. He is imaginative, creative and has a good appreciation of the finer things in life. He has an easy-going nature and prefers to live in a relaxed and pressure-free environment. He hates any sort of discord or unpleasantness and does not like to be bound by a strict routine or rigid timetable. The Goat is not one to be hurried against his will but, despite his seemingly relaxed approach to life, he is something of a perfectionist and when he starts work on a project he is certain to give of his best.

The Goat usually prefers to work in a team rather than on his own. He likes to have the support and encouragement of others and if left to deal with matters on his own he can get very worried and tends to view things rather pessimistically. Wherever possible the Goat will leave major decision-making to others while he concentrates on his own pursuits. If, however, he feels particularly strongly about a certain matter or has to defend his position in any way, he will act with great fortitude and precision.

The Goat has a very persuasive nature and often uses his considerable charm to get his own way. He can, however, be rather hesitant about letting his true feelings be known and if he were prepared to be more forthright he would do much better as a result.

The Goat tends to have a quiet, somewhat reserved nature but when he is in company he likes he can often become the centre of attention. He can be highly amusing, a marvellous host at parties and a superb entertainer. Whenever the spotlight falls on the Goat, his adrenalin starts to flow and he can be assured of giving a sparkling performance, particularly if he is allowed to use his creative skills in any way.

Of all the signs in the Chinese zodiac, the Goat is probably the most gifted artistically. Whether it is in the theatre, literature, music or art, the Goat is certain to make a lasting impression. He is a born creator and is rarely happier than when occupied in some artistic pursuit. But even in this, the Goat does well to work with others rather than on his own. He needs inspiration and a guiding influence, but when he has found his true *métier*, he can often receive widespread acclaim and recognition.

In addition to his liking for the arts, the Goat is usually quite religious and often has a deep interest in nature, animals and the countryside. The Goat is also fairly athletic and there are many who have excelled in some form of sporting activity.

Although the Goat is not particularly materialistic or concerned about finance, he will find that he will usually be lucky in financial matters and will rarely be short of the necessary funds to tide himself over. He is, however, rather indulgent and tends to spend his money as soon as he receives it rather than make provision for the future.

The Goat usually leaves home when he is young but he will always maintain strong links with his parents and the other members of his family. He is also rather nostalgic and is well known for keeping mementoes of his childhood and souvenirs of places that he has visited. His home will not be particularly tidy but he knows where everything is and it will also be scrupulously clean.

Affairs of the heart are particularly important to the Goat and he will often have many romances before he finally settles down. Although the Goat is fairly adaptable, he prefers to live in a secure and stable environment and he will find that he is best suited to those born under the signs of the Tiger, Horse, Monkey, Pig and Rabbit. He can also establish a good relationship with the Dragon, Snake, Rooster and another Goat, but he may find the Ox and Dog a little too serious for his liking. Neither will he care particularly for the Rat's rather thrifty ways.

The lady Goat devotes all her time and energy to the needs of her family. She has excellent taste in home furnishings and often uses her considerable artistic skills to make clothes for herself and her children. She takes great care over her appearance and can be most attractive to the opposite sex. Although she is not the most well-organized of people, her engaging manner and delightful sense of humour creates a favourable impression wherever she goes. She is also a good cook and usually gets much pleasure from gardening and outdoor pursuits.

The Goat can win friends easily and people generally feel relaxed in his company. He has a kind and understanding nature and although he can occasionally be stubborn, he can, with the right support and encouragement, live a happy and very satisfying life. The more he can use his creative skills, the happier he will be.

The Five Different Types of Goat

In addition to the 12 signs of the Chinese zodiac, there are five elements, and these have a strengthening or moderating influence on the sign. The effects of the five elements on the Goat are described below, together with the years in which the elements were exercising their influence. Therefore all Goats born in 1931 and 1991 are Metal Goats, those born in 1943 are Water Goats, and so on.

Metal Goat: 1931, 1991
This Goat is thorough and conscientious in all that he does and is capable of doing very well in his chosen profession. Despite his confident manner, he can be a great worrier and he would find it a help to discuss his worries with others rather than keep them to himself. He is loyal to his family and employers and will have a small group of extremely good friends. He has good artistic taste and is usually highly skilled in some aspect of the arts. He is often a collector of antiques and his home will be very tastefully furnished.

Water Goat: 1943
The Water Goat is very popular and makes friends with remarkable ease. He is good at spotting opportunities but does not always have the necessary confidence to follow them through. He likes to have security both in his home life and at work and does not take kindly to change. He is articulate, has a good sense of humour and is usually very good with children.

Wood Goat: 1895, 1955
This Goat is generous, kind-hearted and always eager to please. He usually has a large circle of friends and involves himself in a wide variety of different activities. He has a very trusting nature but he can sometimes give in to the demands of others a little too easily and it would be in his own interests if he were to stand his ground a little more

often. He is usually lucky in financial matters and, like the Water Goat, is very good with children.

Fire Goat: 1907, 1967
This Goat usually knows what he wants in life and he often uses his considerable charm and persuasive personality in order to achieve his aims. He can sometimes let his imagination run away with him and has a tendency to ignore matters which are not to his liking. He is rather extravagant in his spending and would do well to exercise a little more care when dealing with financial matters. He has a lively personality, has many friends, and loves attending parties and social occasions.

Earth Goat: 1919, 1979
This Goat has a very considerate and caring nature. He is particularly loyal to his family and friends and invariably creates a favourable impression wherever he goes. He is reliable and conscientious in his work but he finds it difficult to save and never likes to deprive himself of any little luxury which he might fancy. He has numerous interests and is often very well read. He usually gets much pleasure from following the activities of various members of his family.

Prospects for the Goat in 1994

The Chinese New Year starts on 10 February 1994. Until then, the old year, the Year of the Rooster, is still making its presence felt.

The Year of the Rooster (23 January 1993 to 9 February 1994) will have been a generally busy and constructive year for the Goat. He will have made steady progress over the year and many Goats will have seen significant changes taking place. Some will have moved while others will have changed their work or seen changes in their personal circumstances.

For what remains of the Year of the Rooster, the Goat needs to adapt to any changes that have taken place and actively pursue his own interests. For the determined Goat, much can be achieved at this time but a lot does depend upon his willingness to assert himself. He will also find that change can often lead to new opportunities and in the closing stages of the year he would do well to look for ways in which he can improve upon his present position. November, December and January are all positive months for the Goat.

There are, however, two areas where the Goat does need to exercise care and this particularly applies to the closing stages of the year. The Goat could have been involved in considerable expense in 1993 and in what remains of the Rooster year he does need to exercise restraint in his spending. To stretch his resources too far could cause problems later.

The other area concerns his relations with others. If, over the course of the year, the Goat has experienced difficulties with some of those around him, this could be an ideal time to sort these out. By taking the initiative and showing a willingness to resolve any outstanding differences, the Goat will not only ease any discord that may exist but will also win the respect of others and this will be very much to his future advantage.

Generally, however, the end of the Rooster year is a favourable time for the Goat and, in addition to the progress he will make in many of his activities, he can also look forward to having some pleasing times with his family and friends.

The Year of the Dog starts on 10 February 1994 and is going to be a challenging year for the Goat. Over the course of the year he may find that some of his plans have to be changed or that certain events do not work out as he would have liked. However, while there are some difficult aspects to his chart, the year will certainly not be without its successes. It is a year for consolidation, for gaining experience, and a year from which the Goat will emerge a stronger and wiser person. His accomplishments over the year will be an important contributory factor to the progress and success he will make in the next few years.

During the Dog year the Goat should continue to set about his various activities to the best of his abilities. However, he would be wise to keep his rather capricious nature in check. It is not a good year for suddenly changing his mind, for taking risks or for jumping from one activity to another. The Goat needs to concentrate on specific objectives and avoid getting involved in more matters than he can sensibly handle at any one time. This is a year for modest and steady progress rather than for being over-ambitious or taking risks.

If the Goat does meet with opposition to any of his plans, he would do well to look at the reasons why and find ways of remedying the problem. Indeed, by looking closely at what he wants to achieve, he can strengthen and improve his plans and this can be to his long-term advantage.

The Goat will also need to exercise a certain amount of patience over the year. In some matters, he may be too anxious for quick results or be trying to achieve things without the proper preparation. In 1994 time is on the Goat's side, and while he may experience set-backs and delays, the work that he carries out and his accomplishments over the year will provide a useful base for the considerable progress he will make in the next few years.

Throughout the year all Goats, whether in work or seeking work, would do well to pursue any opportunities that they see. However, one of the most important factors in 1994 is for the Goat to add to his skills and to gain experience. If he is able to do this, he will do much to enhance his career and future prospects.

This year the Goat will need to exercise care in financial matters. Providing he is prudent and careful all will be well, but if he takes risks or enters into speculative ventures then he could end up the loser. This is just not a year when the Goat can afford to take risks or be too lavish with his spending.

He can, however, look forward to a very satisfying home life over the year. His family and friends will be supportive and encourage him in his various activities. However, in return, the Goat should be open about his plans and seek support and advice for anything that he intends to do. If he neglects to do this and automatically assumes that he has the support of others or ignores advice he is given, he could find strains developing with those around him. This is very much a year when the Goat needs to work closely with others – as indeed many Goats prefer to do – rather than adopting an independent and go-it-alone attitude.

Socially, 1994 will be a generally favourable year and many Goats can look forward to leading a busy and fulfilling social life. The opportunities for building up new friendships and for romance are good, especially in the summer and autumn months.

The Goat will also obtain much satisfaction and pleasure from his interests over the year. These will help to take his mind off everyday pressures as well as being most beneficial for him – especially if they involve him in outdoor or creative activities. If he does not have an interest he can pursue in his spare time he would do well to consider taking one up.

While 1994 may not be the smoothest of years for the Goat, it need not be a bad one. Provided he remains realistic in his undertakings and does not attempt to achieve too much all at once, he can make steady progress. Also, while he may have some problems to overcome, he will certainly not find these insurmountable and in some respects the difficulties could turn out to be blessings in disguise. By looking for ways to surmount any obstacles, the Goat will emerge from the year a wiser, stronger and more experienced person and this can only be to his future advantage. The more challenging aspects in his chart will gradually weaken as the year progresses and from the late summer onwards the Goat can look forward to a general improvement in his situation, an improvement which will continue for the next two years.

As far as the different types of Goat are concerned, 1994 will be a relatively quiet year for the **Metal Goat**. He will lead a pleasant domestic and social life and can look forward to some most enjoyable times with his family and friends. He will also obtain considerable pleasure from his various hobbies and if he is able to add to his interests or skills over the year he will find that this will give him much personal satisfaction. In many respects, his level of achievement over the year rests with him: by using his time wisely and constructively he can turn 1994 into a positive and fulfilling year. Although the Metal Goat, like all Goats, does need to be careful about his overall level of expenditure in 1994, he could nevertheless enjoy some financial good fortune and receive a sum of money from an unexpected source over the year. He does, however, need to exercise care when dealing with important forms or bureaucratic matters. A missed detail or an oversight could take some time to sort out and possibly involve him in some additional expense. If the Metal Goat does have any problems to deal with over the year, he would do well to seek the advice of others rather than deal with the problem single-handed. Generally, however, this will be a reasonable year for the Metal Goat and the summer months in particular are likely to be memorable and most enjoyable.

The **Water Goat** is not one who particularly enjoys change, but over the year he will see several changes taking place. These could concern his work, his accommodation or personal situation, and while some of the changes that occur are outside his control and could cause him moments of anxiety, many of the events that take place will work out to his long-term advantage. This particularly applies if the Water Goat has been stuck in a rut or has been frustrated by his lack of progress in recent years. The changes will present new opportunities and help stimulate him into taking positive and constructive action. They will also help to focus his attention on his present position and what he would like to accomplish in the near future. All this can have a significant and beneficial effect on the Water Goat. From changes, set-backs and disappointments, he should look for new opportunities to pursue – they will certainly be there and by acting boldly and wisely he can turn an indifferent year into one which will have a lasting and beneficial effect on his future. Care is, however, needed in financial matters and the Water Goat should be particularly wary about committing money that he can ill afford to lose to risky ventures. He will, however, obtain much support and pleasure from his family and friends, and while he may not travel great distances in 1994, if he is able to get away for some short breaks at different times during the year he will find these particularly beneficial for him. October and November are likely to be two important and significant months for him.

This will be a generally pleasant year for the **Wood Goat**. He will be much in demand with his family and friends and can look forward to an enjoyable domestic and social life. The year will, however, be quite busy for him and he would do well to ask for assistance if he feels under pressure. Those around him want to help and see him succeed and the Wood Goat would do well to remember that support is at hand if required. He will make steady progress in his work but it is not a suitable year to initiate sudden change or to take risks, either in business or financial matters. If, however, he is able to extend his skills or qualifications in any way he will find that this will do much to improve his long-term prospects. With the generally busy and demanding life that the Wood Goat leads, it is important that he does set some time aside for his hobbies and interests, especially anything that would allow him to use his creative flair or that gives him a break from his everyday activities. Also, if he tends to be reliant on fast or convenience food, the Wood Goat would do well to consider switching to a more balanced diet – he will notice that in time this will do much to improve his well-being. The travelling that he undertakes over the year will go well and he can look forward to some most enjoyable holidays and breaks over the year.

Although not all the events of the year will be to the **Fire Goat**'s liking, it can still be quite a constructive and rewarding time for him. In his work the Fire Goat should concentrate on specific objectives and, if possible, add to his skills and experience. He would also do well to promote his talents and pursue any tempting opportunities that he sees. Admittedly, not all his efforts are likely to be successful and he could meet with opposition to some of his plans, but over the year he will build up valuable experience and this can only be to his future good. If he encounters any opposition to his plans he should look at the reasons why and learn from and rectify any mistakes he may have made. In many respects, the events that occur over the year will strengthen his character, focus his attention on ways he can improve upon his present position and prepare him for the significant advances he will make in the latter part of 1994 and in 1995. The Fire Goat will lead a busy and enjoyable domestic life over the year and he is likely to be much in demand with his family and friends. Should he find himself in a disagreement with anyone it would be in his interests to show himself flexible and conciliatory. To remain intransigent over any matter and reluctant to consider the views of others could result in tension and unhappiness and even hamper his progress. Generally, however, 1994 will be a significant year for the Fire Goat and the experience he gains will serve him well in the next few years.

This will be a varied year for the **Earth Goat**, and one in which he is likely to give much thought both to his present position and to his future. In this he would be wise to talk to those around him and to seek their views. However, if he does have to take any important decisions over the year, he should resist any pressure that others may place on him to take action against his better judgement. Time is on his side and the Earth Goat must be sure in his own mind that any major decision he takes is what he himself desires. Once he has made up his mind then he can proceed with confidence. Those Earth Goats involved in education will find that their work will go well and provided the Earth Goat continues to set about his studies in his usual conscientious manner, his efforts will be well rewarded. Socially, this will be a good year and many Earth Goats will make some new and very good friends over the year. The Earth Goat will also obtain considerable enjoyment from his hobbies and could find that one of his interests could prove quite lucrative for him. If he is able to contact those who share his interests, perhaps by joining a local society or club, he will find that this will not only add to the enjoyment of his interest but increase his circle of friends. He will also obtain much pleasure from outdoor pursuits over the year and activities such as sport, gardening or walking are likely to prove most enjoyable for him.

Famous Goats

Dame Peggy Ashcroft, Isaac Asimov, Jane Austen, Anne Bancroft, Boris Becker, Ian Botham, Elkie Brooks, John le Carré, Nat 'King' Cole, Catherine Deneuve, John Denver, Sir Arthur Conan Doyle, Umberto Eco, Douglas Fairbanks, Bobby Fischer, Dame Margot Fonteyn, Anna Ford, Paul Gascoigne, Paul Michael Glaser, Sharon Gless, Mikhail Gorbachev, Larry Hagman, George Harrison, Sir Edmund Hillary, Hulk Hogan, Julio Iglesias, Mick Jagger, Paul Keating, Ben Kingsley, David Kossoff, Doris Lessing, Peter Lilley, Franz Liszt, John Major, Michelangelo, Cliff

Michelmore, Joni Mitchell, Edwin Moses, Frank Muir, Rupert Murdoch, Mussolini, Leonard Nimoy, Robert de Niro, Oliver North, Des O'Connor, Lord Olivier, Michael Palin, Cecil Parkinson, Javier Perez de Cuellar, Alain Prost, Keith Richards, Sir Malcolm Sargent, Mike Smith, Freddie Starr, Lord Tebbit, Leslie Thomas, Mark Twain, Rudolph Valentino, Vangelis, Lech Walesa, Barbara Walters, John Wayne, Tuesday Weld, Fay Weldon, Bruce Willis, Debra Winger, Paul Young.

The Monkey

2 February 1908 to	21 January 1909	*Earth Monkey*
20 February 1920 to	7 February 1921	*Metal Monkey*
6 February 1932 to	25 January 1933	*Water Monkey*
25 January 1944 to	12 February 1945	*Wood Monkey*
12 February 1956 to	30 January 1957	*Fire Monkey*
30 January 1968 to	16 February 1969	*Earth Monkey*
16 February 1980 to	4 February 1981	*Metal Monkey*
4 February 1992 to	22 January 1993	*Water Monkey*

The Personality of the Monkey

> Man is what he believes.
> – *Anton Chekhov: a Monkey.*

The Monkey is born under the sign of fantasy. He is imaginative, inquisitive, and loves to keep an eye on everything that is going on around him. He is never backward in offering advice or trying to sort out the problems of others. He likes to be helpful and his advice is invariably sensible and reliable.

The Monkey is intelligent, well-read and always eager to learn. He has an extremely good memory and there are many Monkeys who have made particularly good linguists. The Monkey is also a convincing talker and enjoys taking part in discussions and debates. His friendly, self-assured manner can be very persuasive and he usually has little trouble in winning people round to his way of thinking – it is for this reason that the Monkey often excels in politics and public speaking. He is also particularly adept in PR work, teaching and any job which involves selling.

The Monkey can, however, be crafty, cunning and occasionally dishonest, and he will seize on any opportunity to make a quick gain or outsmart his opponents. He has so much charm and guile that people often don't realize what he is up to until it is too late. But despite his resourceful nature, the Monkey does run the risk of outsmarting even himself. He has so much confidence in his abilities that he rarely listens to advice or is prepared to accept help from anyone. The Monkey likes to help others but prefers to rely on his own judgement when dealing with his own affairs.

Another characteristic of the Monkey is that he is extremely good at solving problems and has a happy knack of extricating himself (and others) from the most hopeless of positions. He is the master of self-preservation.

With so many diverse talents the Monkey is able to make considerable sums of money, but he does like to enjoy life and will think nothing of spending his money on some exotic holiday or luxury which he has had his eye on. He can, however, become very envious if someone else has got what he wants.

The Monkey is an original thinker and, despite his love of company, he cherishes his independence. He has to have the freedom to act as he wants and any Monkey who feels hemmed in or bound by too many restrictions can soon become unhappy. Likewise, if anything becomes too boring or monotonous, he soon loses interest and turns his attention to something else. The Monkey lacks persistence and this can often hamper his progress. He is also easily distracted, a tendency which all Monkeys should try to overcome. The Monkey should concentrate on one thing at a time and by doing so will almost certainly achieve more in the long run.

The Monkey is a good organizer and, even though he may

behave slightly erratically at times, he will invariably have some plan at the back of his mind. On the odd occasion when his plans do not quite work out, he is usually quite happy to shrug his shoulders and put it down to experience. He will rarely make the same mistake twice and throughout his life he will try his hand at many things.

The Monkey likes to impress and is rarely without followers or admirers. There are many who are attracted to him by his good looks, his sense of humour, or simply because he instils so much confidence.

Monkeys usually marry young and for it to be a success their partner must allow them time to pursue their many interests and the opportunity to indulge in their love of travel. The Monkey has to have variety in his life and is especially well-suited to those born under the sociable and outgoing signs of the Rat, Dragon, Pig and Goat. The Ox, Rabbit, Snake and Dog will also be enchanted by the Monkey's resourceful and outgoing nature, but the Monkey is likely to exasperate the Rooster and Horse, and the Tiger will have little patience for the Monkey's tricks. A relationship between two Monkeys will also work well – they will understand each other and be able to assist each other in their various enterprises.

The lady Monkey is intelligent, extremely observant and a shrewd judge of character. Her opinions and views are often highly valued, and having such a persuasive nature, she invariably gets her own way. The lady Monkey has many interests and involves herself in a wide variety of activities. She pays great attention to her appearance, is an elegant dresser, and likes to take particular care over her hair. She can also be a most caring and doting parent and will have many good and loyal friends.

Provided the Monkey can curb his desire to take part in all that is going on around him and concentrate on one thing at a time, he can usually achieve what he wants in life. Should he suffer any disappointments, he is bound to bounce back. The Monkey is a survivor and his life is usually both colourful and very eventful.

The Five Different Types of Monkey

In addition to the 12 signs of the Chinese zodiac, there are five elements and these have a strengthening or moderating influence on the sign. The effects of the five elements on the Monkey are described below, together with the years in which the elements were exercising their influence. Therefore all Monkeys born in 1920 and 1980 are Metal Monkeys, those born in 1932 and 1992 are Water Monkeys, and so on.

Metal Monkey: 1920, 1980
The Metal Monkey is very strong-willed. He sets about everything he does with a dogged determination and often prefers to work independently rather than with others. He is ambitious, wise and confident, and is certainly not afraid of hard work. He is very astute in financial matters and usually chooses his investments well. Despite his somewhat independent nature, the Metal Monkey enjoys attending parties and social occasions and is particularly warm and caring towards his loved ones.

Water Monkey: 1932, 1992
The Water Monkey is versatile, determined and perceptive. He also has more discipline than some of the other Monkeys and is prepared to work towards a certain goal rather than be distracted by something else. He is not always open about his true intentions and when questioned can be particularly evasive. He can be sensitive to criticism but also very persuasive and usually has little trouble in getting others to fall in with his plans. He has a very good understanding of human nature and relates well to others.

Wood Monkey: 1944
This Monkey is efficient, methodical and extremely conscientious. He is also highly imaginative and is always trying to capitalize on new ideas or learning new skills. Occasionally his enthusiasm can get the better of him and he can get very agitated when things do not quite work out as he had hoped. He does, however, have a very adventurous streak in him and is not afraid of taking risks. He also loves travel. He is usually held in great esteem by his friends and colleagues.

Fire Monkey: 1896, 1956
The Fire Monkey is intelligent, full of vitality, and has no trouble in commanding the respect of others. He is imaginative and has wide interests, although sometimes these can distract him from more useful and profitable work. He is very competitive and always likes to be involved in everything that is going on. He can be stubborn if he does not get his own way and he sometimes tries to indoctrinate those who are less strong-willed than himself. The Fire Monkey is a lively character, popular with the opposite sex and extremely loyal to his partner.

Earth Monkey: 1908, 1968
The Earth Monkey tends to be studious and well-read, and can become quite distinguished in his chosen line of work. He is less outgoing than some of the other types of Monkey and prefers quieter and more solid pursuits. He has high principles, a very caring nature, and can be most generous to those less fortunate than himself. He is usually successful in handling financial matters and can become very wealthy in old age. He has a calming influence on those around him and is respected and well liked by those he meets. He is, however, especially careful about whom he lets into his confidence.

Prospects for the Monkey in 1994

The Chinese New Year starts on 10 February 1994. Until then, the old year, the Year of the Rooster, is still making its presence felt.

The Year of the Rooster (23 January 1993 to 9 February 1994) will have been a generally pleasant and reasonable year for the Monkey. He is likely to have made progress in his work and this positive trend will continue to the very end of the Rooster year.

For what remains of this Chinese year, the Monkey should continue to seek out opportunities that are available to him and promote his talents and skills. This particularly applies to those Monkeys seeking work or a new position. By acting positively and determinedly, the Monkey can make great progress in the closing stages of the Rooster year, with January in particular being a good month.

The Monkey is likely to have led a busy and possibly expensive social life in the Rooster year, and again this trend will continue to the very end of the year. Around the Christmas and New Year holidays the Monkey will be invited to several parties and functions and these will not only prove enjoyable but will also widen his circle of friends quite considerably. For those Monkeys who are unattached, the prospects for making new friends and for romance is particularly good in the closing months of the year.

The Monkey does, however, need to be careful in his spending. The Year of the Rooster is invariably an expensive year for the Monkey and it is not a year when he can afford to take risks or be too extravagant. To borrow or stretch his resources too far could cause problems later and it is a warning that the Monkey would do well to heed!

Some Monkeys may also have had to contend with a few domestic problems in the Rooster year. These could have been caused because the Monkey has been too preoccupied with his own concerns. If he feels that this has been the case, he would do well to remedy the situation by making a conscious effort to involve himself more in the activities of those around him. If he can do this, he will notice a pleasing improvement taking place in his relations with others. Alternatively, if he has had a difference of opinion with someone, the latter part of the year could be an ideal time to sort the problem out and anything constructive that the Monkey can do to improve any strained relations that he may have will be time well spent.

Generally, however, the closing stages of the Rooster year will be a positive and enjoyable time for the Monkey and he will be pleased with how much he is able to accomplish.

The Year of the Dog begins on 10 February 1994 and is going to be a challenging year for the Monkey. Some aspects of his life will go well, but in other areas he needs to exercise care.

Throughout the year the Monkey should avoid taking unnecessary risks or involving himself in too many projects all at one time. In his work he should stick to areas which he is familiar with rather than committing himself to undertakings of which he has little experience or knowledge. He should also not be over-ambitious in his activities. By concentrating on specific areas he can make progress, but by over-committing himself or by taking risks, the Monkey could find himself in difficulties.

The Monkey should also make sure that he has the support of those around him before taking any important decisions or actions. Without this he could find himself isolated and lacking the support he needs. It would also be in his interests to listen carefully to others over the year and keep tabs on all that is going on around him. In 1994 the Monkey will need to work with others rather than retain an independent attitude. If he does this he can make steady progress in his work or, if he is seeking work or wanting a change in his work, be successful in obtaining a new position. With care and a positive attitude the Monkey can do well.

Should, however, the Monkey experience any problems over the year or find that his plans are not working out as he would like, he would find it helpful to take stock of what is happening and analyse where he is going wrong. This will help him to avoid making the same mistake twice as well as focusing his attention on his present situation. With his resourceful and innovative mind, he should be able to overcome any difficulties that do arise and end the year with some worthy gains to his credit. Generally, however, the Monkey does need to be cautious in his undertakings and, as far as possible, he should plan and think his various commitments and activities out. This is just not a good year for taking risks, acting on the spur of the moment or for embarking on ambitious new projects. In the Dog year the Monkey needs to plan and then proceed carefully and cautiously.

This need for caution also extends itself to financial matters. The Monkey should avoid stretching his resources too far or taking risks with his money. He should also be wary of lending to others as he could experience difficulty in getting the loan repaid. If, however, the Monkey carries out a review of his financial situation and cuts down on any outgoings that might no longer be essential, he will be surprised at what a difference can be made. This would be particularly useful for any Monkeys who may have been experiencing financial problems in recent times.

Although this is a generally testing year for the Monkey, he can take comfort from his family and friends. They are there to support and advise him and while the Monkey may not be as forthcoming as some when discussing his own concerns, he would be very much helped by being more open in discussing any problems or worries that he has. Likewise, he should make every effort to involve those around him in his various activities; again, he will be heartened by the interest, support and encouragement that others are prepared to give him.

The Monkey will lead a generally pleasant social life over

the year and while there will be opportunities for the unattached Monkey to meet others, he should be wary of rushing into any commitment after only a short time. He will find it better to let a new friendship develop gradually and in its own time. He will also find that this will help to put the friendship on a more secure foundation.

Although there will be many demands on his time over the year, it is important that the Monkey allows himself the opportunity to relax and to have a break from his usual daily activities. He should try to set some regular time aside for his interests and hobbies – if he does not already have a hobby or interest he can devote time to, he would do well to take one up. Some Monkeys might also consider enrolling on a correspondence course or taking a course at a special adult education class. This will not only give them a new interest but could also usefully extend their skills.

The Monkey will also find that if he is able to take some short breaks at different times of the year these will be most beneficial and enjoyable for him.

Although not all the events of the year will work out in the Monkey's favour, it can still be a constructive year for him. Provided he does not take unnecessary risks or act without the support of others he can make a reasonable amount of progress. Also, by examining the reasons for any set-backs that occur, he can learn from any mistakes he may have made and emerge from the year a wiser and more experienced person. In all his activities it would be helpful for him to try to overcome his rather secretive nature and be more open and forthcoming with others.

In 1994 the Monkey will learn a lot about himself, his attitudes, his values and his relations with others. In future years he will be able to put this knowledge and experience to good use.

As far as the different types of Monkey are concerned, 1994 will be a variable year for the **Metal Monkey**. Over the course of the year he may have to overcome a few problems and also rethink some of his plans. These set-backs need not be serious but the Metal Monkey would do well to show a certain amount of flexibility in his attitude. Sometimes he can be rather stubborn as well as preferring to retain a certain independence in his actions and in 1994 such an attitude could work against him. Over the year, the Metal Monkey should show himself willing to consider the viewpoints of others and be prepared to adapt and make the best of new situations as they arise. If he can do this, the year will generally prove satisfying and pleasant for him. Also, if the Metal Monkey has to take any important decisions he would do well to seek the views of those around them and, while he may not necessarily agree with all they say, he should remember that they are speaking with his best interests at heart. The Metal Monkey also needs to exercise care in financial matters and should avoid stretching his resources too far. Socially, however, this will be a busy and enjoyable year for him and he will get much enjoyment from any travelling that he undertakes and also from his various interests. Outdoor activities in particular are likely to give him much pleasure.

This will be a significant year for the **Water Monkey**. Over the course of the year he will take several important decisions which will have a bearing on his long-term future. In making these decisions, the Water Monkey would do well to take his time and also not allow himself to be pushed or manoeuvred into doing anything which he himself is not happy about. He must first be sure in his own mind that any decision or action he takes is what he wants and what is right for him. Once he is satisfied, he can then proceed with confidence. Throughout the year, however, the Water Monkey should keep his aims and expectations on a realistic level – to try to be too ambitious and reach for almost impossible goals will only lead to disappointment. He also needs to be careful in financial matters and be wary of investing any spare money he has in risky ventures or in areas he knows little about. If he is not careful, he could suffer financial loss. The Water Monkey can, however, look forward to some memorable times with his family and friends. He will also be able to take particular delight in the activities and achievements of a younger relation. Although this will be quite a busy year for the Water Monkey, he would do well to set some time aside and take up a completely new interest; perhaps one that intrigued him in the past but he never had time to investigate. He could find a new interest mentally stimulating as well as uncovering talents that he never realized he had!

Although not all the events of the year may be to the **Wood Monkey**'s liking, this can still be an important and valuable year for him. Throughout the year he should continue to set about his various activities in his usual methodical way. Admittedly, he may have to face delays and set-backs over the year, but providing he is not deflected from his general aim, he will still be able to make steady progress. Wood Monkeys who are seeking work or who would like a change of work will find a persevering attitude will bring results. For the determined Wood Monkey, this can be a constructive year and the experience he gains (both good and bad) will help prepare him for the substantial progress and more positive times that lie ahead for him in the next few years. The Wood Monkey's family will be a great source of pride to him and many Wood Monkeys will take part in a memorable family celebration over the year. The Wood Monkey will also be appreciative of the support and advice those close to him are able to give and if there is any matter that is troubling him, he would do well to seek their advice. In view of the many demands and pressures that the Wood Monkey will face over the year, it is important that he takes good care of himself. He should try to make sure that he eats a balanced diet, exercises well and allows himself time to rest and properly unwind at regular intervals. He could find swimming, additional walking or some other suitable exercise particularly beneficial for him.

This will be an interesting and varied year for the **Fire Monkey**. The Fire Monkey often does well when facing new challenges or when dealing with any matters that catch his imagination. He has an innovative and determined nature and these two qualities will serve him well over the year. By remaining vigilant and looking for opportunities to pursue, the Fire Monkey can make considerable progress. Admittedly, not everything that the Fire Monkey attempts will be successful and he could experience several set-backs over the year, but out of any disappointments that occur, new opportunities will emerge, and these are the opportunities that the Fire Monkey would do well to pursue. Also, the experience he gains will contribute to the significant progress he will make in the next few years. The Fire Monkey's domestic and social life will be generally settled and content but it would be in his interests not to assume that he has the automatic support of others or to be too demanding. Throughout the year the Fire Monkey does need to listen carefully to the views of those around him and make sure that he has the necessary support before embarking on any new enterprise. The Fire Monkey will enjoy the travelling that he undertakes over the year and he is also likely to obtain much satisfaction from any outdoor or creative activities that he pursues over the year.

This will be a reasonable year for the **Earth Monkey** and while not everything may work out in the manner he would like, he will still be generally satisfied with his accomplishments over the year. In his work he could take on new responsibilities or be successful in obtaining a completely different type of job. He should also view any positive changes that occur in his work as valuable opportunities to gain experience. The additional skills he is able to acquire will prove important to him in the future. Some Earth Monkeys will also change their accommodation over the year and while this could occupy much of the Earth Monkey's time, he will find such a change will lead to new friends and also some new openings for him to pursue. Personally, he may also have good cause for a celebration in 1994 and, indeed, many Earth Monkeys will see an addition to their family over the year. However, with the many demands on his time, it is important that the Earth Monkey does not commit himself to too many undertakings all at the same time and as far as possible spreads his commitments out. He will also find it beneficial if he set some regular time aside for his own recreational interests, preferably doing something unrelated to his usual daytime activity. October and November will be two favourable months for him and generally the second half of the year will be a more fulfilling and rewarding time for him than the earlier part of the year.

Famous Monkeys

Michael Aspel, George Baker, Bobby Ball, J.M. Barrie, David Bellamy, Jacqueline Bisset, Bjorn Borg, Frank Bough, Faith Brown, Yul Brynner, Julius Caesar, Marti Caine, Princess Caroline of Monaco, Johnny Cash, Roy Castle, Sebastian Coe, John Constable, Alistair Cooke, Joan Crawford, Charles Dickens, Jonathan Dimbleby, Jason Donovan, Kenny Everett, Mia Farrow, Michael Fish, F. Scott Fitzgerald, Ian Fleming, Dick Francis, Paul Gauguin, Luke Goss, Matt Goss, Jerry Hall, Tom Hanks, Roy Hattersley, Stephen Hendry, Patricia Highsmith, Harry Houdini, Tony Jacklin, P.D. James, Pope John Paul II, Lyndon B. Johnson, Edward Kennedy, Nigel Kennedy, Jonathan King, Gladys Knight, Cyndi Lauper, Lord Lawson, Leo McKern, Walter Matthau, Princess Michael of Kent, Kylie Minogue, Martina Navratilova, Jack Nicklaus, Derek Nimmo, Peter O'Toole, Chris Patten, Mario Puzo, Debbie Reynolds, Tim Rice, Little Richard, Angela Rippon, Diana Ross, Omar Sharif, Wilbur Smith, Koo Stark, Rod Stewart, Michael Stich, Elizabeth Taylor, Graham Taylor, Dame Kiri Te Kanawa, Harry

Truman, Leonardo da Vinci, Brian Walden, Norman Willis, Gary Wilmot, the Duchess of Windsor, Bobby Womack.

The Rooster

22 January 1909 to	9 February 1910	***Earth Rooster***
8 February 1921 to	27 January 1922	***Metal Rooster***
26 January 1933 to	13 February 1934	***Water Rooster***
13 February 1945 to	1 February 1946	***Wood Rooster***
31 January 1957 to	17 February 1958	***Fire Rooster***
17 February 1969 to	5 February 1970	***Earth Rooster***
5 February 1981 to	24 January 1982	***Metal Rooster***
23 January 1993 to	9 February 1994	***Water Rooster***

The Personality of the Rooster

If you create an act, you create a habit. If you create a habit, you create a character. If you create a character, you create destiny.

– André Maurois: a Rooster.

The Rooster is born under the sign of candour. He has a flamboyant and colourful personality and is meticulous in all that he does. He is an excellent organizer and wherever possible likes to plan his various activities well in advance.

The Rooster is highly intelligent and usually very well read. He has a good sense of humour and is an effective and persuasive speaker. He loves discussion and enjoys taking part in any sort of debate. He has no hesitation in speaking his mind and is forthright in his views. He does, however, lack tact and can easily damage his reputation or cause offence by some thoughtless remark or action. The Rooster also has a very volatile nature, and he should always try to avoid acting on the spur of the moment.

The Rooster is usually very dignified in his manner and conducts himself with an air of confidence and authority. He is adept at handling financial matters and, as with most things, he organizes his financial affairs with considerable skill. He chooses his investments well and is capable of achieving great wealth. Most Roosters save or use their money wisely, but there are a few who are the reverse and are notorious spendthrifts. Fortunately, the Rooster has great earning capacity and is rarely without sufficient funds to tide himself over.

Another characteristic of the Rooster is that he invariably carries a notebook or scraps of paper around with him. He is constantly writing himself reminders or noting down important facts lest he forgets – the Rooster cannot abide inefficiency and conducts all his activities in an orderly, precise and methodical manner.

The Rooster is usually very ambitious, but can be unrealistic in some of the things that he hopes to achieve. He occasionally lets his imagination run away with him and, while he does not like any interference in the things that he does, it would be in his own interests if he were to listen to the views of others a little more often. He also does not like criticism, and if he feels anybody is doubting his judgement or prying too closely into his affairs, the Rooster is certain to let his feelings be known. He can also be rather self-centred and stubborn over relatively trivial matters, but to compensate for this he is reliable, honest and trustworthy, and this is very much appreciated by all who come into contact with him.

Roosters born between the hours of five and seven (both at dawn and sundown), tend to be the most extrovert of their sign, but all Roosters like to lead an active social life and enjoy attending parties and big functions. The Rooster usually has a wide circle of friends and is able to build up influential contacts with remarkable ease. He often belongs to several clubs and societies and involves himself in a variety of different activities. He is particularly interested in the environment, humanitarian affairs and anything affecting the welfare of others. The Rooster has a very caring nature and will do much to help those less fortunate than himself.

He also gets much pleasure from gardening and, while he may not spend as much time in the garden as he would like, his garden is invariably well-kept and extremely productive.

The Rooster is generally very distinguished in his appearance and, if his job permits, he will wear an official uniform with great pride and dignity. He is not averse to publicity and takes great delight in being the centre of attention. He often does well at PR work or any job which brings him into contact with the media. He also makes a very good teacher.

The lady Rooster leads a varied and interesting life. She involves herself in many different activities and there are some who wonder how she can achieve so much. The lady Rooster often holds very strong views and, like her male counterpart, has no hesitation in speaking her mind or telling others how she thinks things should be done. She is supremely efficient and well-organized and her home is usually very neat and tidy. The lady Rooster has good taste in clothes and usually wears smart but very practical outfits.

The Rooster usually has a large family and as a parent takes a particularly active interest in the education of his children. He is very loyal to his partner and will find that he is especially well-suited to those born under the signs of the Snake, Horse, Ox and Dragon. Provided they do not interfere too much in the Rooster's various activities the Rat, Tiger, Goat and Pig can also establish a good relationship with the Rooster, but two Roosters together are likely to squabble and irritate each other. The rather sensitive Rabbit will find the Rooster a bit too blunt for his liking, and the Rooster will quickly become exasperated by the ever-inquisitive and artful Monkey. The Rooster will also find it difficult to get on with the Dog.

If the Rooster can overcome his volatile nature and exercise more tact in some of the things that he says, he will go far in life. He is capable and talented and will invariably make a lasting – and usually favourable – impression almost everywhere he goes.

The Five Different Types of Rooster

In addition to the 12 signs of the Chinese zodiac, there are five elements and these have a strengthening or moderating influence on the sign. The effects of the five elements on the Rooster are described below, together with the years in which the elements were exercising their influence. Therefore all Roosters born in 1921 and 1981 are Metal Roosters, those born in 1933 and 1993 are Water Roosters, and so on.

Metal Rooster: 1921, 1981
The Metal Rooster is a hard and conscientious worker. He knows exactly what he wants in life and sets about everything he does in a positive and determined manner. He can at times appear abrasive and he would almost certainly do better if he were more willing to reach a compromise with others rather than hold so rigidly to his firmly held beliefs. He is very articulate and most astute when dealing with financial matters. He is loyal to his friends and often devotes much energy to working for the common good.

Water Rooster: 1933, 1993
This Rooster has a very persuasive manner and can easily gain the co-operation of others. He is intelligent, well-read, and gets much enjoyment from taking part in discussions

and debates. He has a seemingly inexhaustible amount of energy and is prepared to work long hours in order to secure what he wants. He can, however, waste much valuable time worrying over minor and inconsequential details. He is approachable, has a good sense of humour, and is highly regarded by others.

Wood Rooster: 1945
The Wood Rooster is honest, reliable and often sets himself high standards. He is ambitious, but also more prepared to work in a team than some of the other types of Rooster. He usually succeeds in life but does have a tendency to get caught up in bureaucratic matters or attempt too many things all at the same time. He has wide interests, likes to travel, and is very considerate and caring towards his family and friends.

Fire Rooster: 1897, 1957
This Rooster is extremely strong-willed. He has many leadership qualities, is an excellent organizer, and is most efficient in his work. Through sheer force of character he often secures his objectives, but he does have a tendency to be very forthright and not always consider the feelings of others. If the Fire Rooster can learn to be more tactful he can often succeed beyond his wildest dreams.

Earth Rooster: 1909, 1969
This Rooster has a deep and penetrating mind. He is extremely efficient, very perceptive, and is particularly astute in business and financial matters. He is also persistent, and once he has set himself an objective, he will rarely allow himself to be deflected from achieving his aim. The Earth Rooster works hard and is held in great esteem by his friends and colleagues. He usually gets much enjoyment from the arts and takes a keen interest in the activities of the various members of his family.

Prospects for the Rooster in 1994

The Chinese New Year starts on 10 February 1994. Until then, the old year, the Year of the Rooster, is still making its presence felt.

The Year of the Rooster (23 January 1993 to 9 February 1994) is the Rooster's own year and a most auspicious and favourable time for him. By pursuing his aims and objectives and by working hard he can make excellent progress. The Rooster year is a year when the Rooster needs to be bold, positive and determined. If he can maintain this attitude, his efforts will be well-rewarded.

In what remains of the Rooster year, the Rooster should promote his talents and skills and pursue any opportunities that he sees. He would also do well to advance any new ideas that he has and start any projects that he might have been considering. These projects can be concerned with his work, his own interests or home improvements, but by setting his plans in motion, the Rooster will not only be satisfied with the results he obtains but pleased that he has done something constructive and positive. The aspects for the Rooster at this time are most encouraging and it is up to him to make the most of them.

Domestically and socially, this will be a happy time for the Rooster. He will be invited to several enjoyable functions in the closing stages of the year and these will give him the opportunity to make some new friends and acquaintances. This can be a splendid time for any Rooster who is lonely or seeking new friends – he would do well to make every effort to go out more and to give himself the opportunity of meeting more people. In the later stages of the Rooster year and in 1994 the Rooster can build up some new and important friendships.

While the closing stages of the Rooster year can be a fulfilling time for the Rooster, there are two areas where he does need to exercise care. Should he find himself involved in any contentious discussion, he would do well to watch that rather candid Rooster tongue of his. To impair his relations with others could undo some of the goodwill which he has built up over the year. Secondly, he needs to deal with any important forms or letters that he receives with great care. An oversight or neglected detail could cause him to waste time that he could be putting to better use. However, 1993 and early 1994 is the Rooster's own year and with the right attitude, effort and luck, his achievements at this time can be quite considerable.

The Year of the Dog starts on 10 February 1994 and is going to be a variable year for the Rooster. Most of his activities will go well, but to make progress the Rooster will need to proceed with a certain amount of care.

In his work, the Rooster will make steady progress. However, it would be best if he concentrated on areas familiar to him rather than devoting time to matters that are new to him or about which he has only limited knowledge. It is not a suitable year for the Rooster to embark on ambitious new projects or to take risks, but providing he is his usual conscientious and meticulous self, he will do well.

The aspects are also favourable for Roosters looking for work and they would do well to pursue any openings that they see. Although they might not always be successful in obtaining the actual position they are seeking, once they are in work they will find that new opportunities will present themselves which had not been available to them before. Also, all Roosters will greatly benefit from the experience that they are able to obtain over the year.

The Rooster will, however, need to exercise care in financial matters in 1994. This is not a year when he can take risks with his money. If he does have any financial problems to deal with over the year, he would do well to look at his outgoings and make whatever modifications he feels necessary. Also, if he intends to make any sizeable purchase over the year, he could save himself a considerable amount of money by checking various sources first.

Domestically, this will be a content and settled year for the Rooster. He can look forward to some splendid times with his family and friends, and should he have any matter that is particularly troubling him, he would do well to seek the opinions of those close to him. His family will be most supportive over the year and the Rooster will be grateful for the encouragement and advice he is given.

Socially, this will also be a busy year for the Rooster and he is likely to attend several memorable functions as well as being much in demand with his friends. This will be a good year for any Rooster who is unattached or seeking new friends: the aspects are most favourable for establishing new friendships and for romance. The Rooster should make every effort to go out more and to give himself the opportunity to meet others. The spring and autumn months will be particularly happy times.

One other area which is well aspected is travel. There will be several opportunities for the Rooster to travel considerable distances in 1994 and the journeys that he undertakes will go well. It is a good year for him to visit friends and relations he has not seen for some time or to visit areas which are new to him. Also, if any Rooster would like to broaden his experience by working in a different country, 1994 would be an ideal year to do this.

While the Rooster's general activities will go well, he will nevertheless have a few niggling problems to overcome. These will not be serious but they could cause him to rethink some of his plans. In tackling any problems that do arise he would do well to seek the advice of those around him and, in case of any disagreements, he should look for compromise rather than confrontation. Also, although the Rooster is usually meticulous in his business and financial undertakings, he should avoid getting involved in any disreputable or dubious schemes over the year. If he does, he could be storing up a lot of trouble for himself and it is a warning the Rooster would do well to heed.

Generally, this will be an important year for the Rooster

and while not everything will work out in his favour, he will gain much valuable experience and wisdom. He should regard problems that occur as challenges to overcome and look for opportunities in any new situations that arise. Providing he is prepared to work hard and concentrate on areas where his main strengths lie, he will make steady progress.

As far as the different types of Rooster are concerned, 1994 will be a quiet and pleasant year for the **Metal Rooster**. He will be able to make useful progress in his various activities as well as obtaining pleasure from his hobbies and interests. Throughout the year, however, it would be better for the Metal Rooster to concentrate on specific areas rather than spread his activities and energies out too widely. By doing so he will obtain more satisfying and worthwhile results. Those Metal Roosters involved in education are also likely to do well and will make good progress. Almost all Metal Roosters will give some thought to their future over the year and in doing so they should listen carefully to the views of others. They should avoid taking any irrevocable decision hastily. Time is on their side and by considering various options, the Metal Rooster can be assured of making the right decision. Socially, 1994 will be an active and enjoyable year and the aspects are also favourable for travel. The Metal Rooster does, however, need to exercise care in financial matters and avoid committing himself to any new undertaking unless he is sure of all the implications. He should also deal with any important correspondence or forms he receives with care. A mistake or oversight could be to his detriment. Generally, however, the Metal Rooster will enjoy 1994 and be pleased with his achievements over the year.

This will be a pleasant and generally satisfying year for the **Water Rooster**. To get the best from it, however, he would do well to give himself some objective to go after. This could be learning a new skill or taking up a new hobby.

By giving himself something practical to aim for he will gain an added impetus to do well and to make the most of his considerable talents and experience. His achievements and rewards over the year can be substantial, but much does depend upon his attitude. The Water Rooster will obtain much enjoyment from outdoor activities and for those Water Roosters who are keen travellers, avid gardeners or sporting enthusiasts, the year will hold many satisfying moments. There will be some splendid opportunities for travel over the year and many Water Roosters will undertake lengthy and interesting journeys in 1994. The Water Rooster's domestic and social life is well aspected and if there is any particular problem that he has to deal with over the year, he would do well to seek the advice of others rather than shoulder the problem all by himself. To give himself undue worry could mar what will otherwise be a generally favourable year for him. It would also be in his interests to keep a close watch on his level of expenditure and avoid getting involved in any highly speculative ventures. This is not a year for taking financial risks.

This can be a successful year for the **Wood Rooster**, provided he sets about his activities in an orderly and methodical way. With his enthusiastic nature and inquisitive mind there is a danger that he could easily get distracted or take on too many commitments all at the same time. In 1994 he should set himself priorities and concentrate on these. To be over-ambitious or over-commit himself could cause problems and lead to less pleasing and satisfying results. To make progress and do well – and the Wood Rooster *can* do well in 1994 – he does need to concentrate on specific objectives. He also needs to exercise care in financial matters and avoid stretching his resources too far. The Wood Rooster's family will be a great source of pleasure to him over the year and he can look forward to leading a content and settled home life. Socially, too, this will be an enjoyable year and the Wood Rooster will find that his circle of friends and acquaintances will increase quite substantially. The Wood Rooster will also enjoy the travelling that he undertakes over the year. Those Wood Roosters who do not get much exercise during the day would do well to consider remedying this by possibly going swimming or walking or taking up some other suitable activity. They will notice an improvement in their well-being if they are able to do this. While 1994 will be a generally positive and fulfilling year for the Wood Rooster, he may still encounter a few problems. These could involve a disagreement with someone or a problem of a bureaucratic nature. In either case, the Wood Rooster should try to deal with the problem as quickly as he can. If not, there is a danger that it could take some time to resolve and mar what will otherwise be a constructive and fulfilling year for him.

This will be a variable year for the **Fire Rooster**. He may find that some of his plans do not work out in the manner he had hoped and he could face delays, opposition or a series of small and niggling problems. Although this could cause the Fire Rooster to feel frustrated and at times disheartened, any difficulties will be short-lived and could even work in his long-term favour. By overcoming the problems that arise, the Fire Rooster will gain valuable experience and also learn where he might have made mistakes in the past. The problems could also help focus his attention on his present situation and help him to rethink and strengthen his future plans. In many ways 1994 is a year for taking stock of his present position and for planning and preparing for the future. The Fire Rooster will make good progress in his work and many will see a change in the nature of their duties or, for those seeking work or a new job, a more satisfying position. The Fire Rooster does, however, need to be careful in financial matters over the year and should avoid stretching his resources too far. He can look forward to having some enjoyable times with his family and friends, and those around him will be most supportive throughout the year. He will also take considerable pride and pleasure in the achievements of a younger member of the family and any assistance that he can give will be thoroughly appreciated. The Fire Rooster will enjoy any travelling that he undertakes over the year and if he is able to take some short breaks at different times of the year he will find these most beneficial for him.

This will be a reasonably good year for the **Earth Rooster**. He is likely to do well in his work and, providing he continues to set about his duties in his usual efficient and conscientious manner, he will make satisfying progress. Those Earth Roosters seeking work would do well to pursue any opportunities that they see and, if possible, try to widen their skills. By remaining positive and determined, all Earth Roosters can achieve pleasing results, but it does require effort and application on their part. March and April could be two particularly fortunate months for the Earth Rooster. He does, however, need to be careful in financial matters over the year and should avoid getting involved in any risky or speculative venture. Also, if he is involved in any major transaction – particularly if he changes his accommodation over the year – he needs to keep a close watch on all the costs involved. Without proper care he could be involved in more expense than is necessary and this could lead to problems. The Earth Rooster will, however, lead a pleasant domestic life and many will have good reason for a family celebration over the year. The Earth Rooster's social life, too, is likely to be enjoyable and for those who are unattached, the aspects are highly favourable for romance and for making new friends. Travel is also favourably aspected and the Earth Rooster will enjoy the journeys that he undertakes over the year. Although this will be a generally satisfying and pleasant year for the Earth Rooster, it will also be a demanding one for him. In view of this, he will find it helpful to set some regular time aside to devote to his hobbies or interests or to take up a new recreational pursuit. He will find that this will not only give him many satisfying moments but also provide him with a new and valuable source of relaxation.

Famous Roosters

Kate Adie, Dame Janet Baker, Severiano Ballesteros, Michael Bentine, Lloyd Bentsen, Dirk Bogarde, Barbara Taylor Bradford, Julian Bream, Richard Briers, Michael Caine, Jasper Carrott, Enrico Caruso, Christopher Cazenove, Eric Clapton, Joan Collins, Roger Daltry, Dickie Davies, Steve Davis, Les Dawson, Cathy Dennis, the Duke of Edinburgh, Gloria Estefan, Douglas Fairbanks Jnr., Nick Faldo, Bryan Ferry, Errol Flynn, Stephen Fry, Steffi Graf, Richard Harris, Deborah Harry, Goldie Hawn, Katherine Hepburn, James Herbert, Michael Heseltine, Diane Keaton, Tom King, Bernhard Langer, D.H. Lawrence, Martyn Lewis, David Livingstone, Ken Livingstone, David McCallum, Jayne Mansfield, Steve Martin, James Mason, W. Somerset Maugham, Van Morrison, Paul Nicholas, Barry Norman, Kim Novak, Yoko Ono, Donny Osmond, Dolly Parton, Michelle Pfeiffer, Roman Polanski, Priscilla Presley, Nancy Reagan, Joan Rivers, Bobby Robson, Sir Harry Secombe, George Segal, Carly Simon, Johann Strauss, Jacqueline Susann, Jayne Torvill, Sir Peter Ustinov, Richard Wagner.

The Dog

10 February 1910 to	29 January 1911	*Metal Dog*
28 January 1922 to	15 February 1923	*Water Dog*
14 February 1934 to	3 February 1935	*Wood Dog*
2 February 1946 to	21 January 1947	*Fire Dog*
18 February 1958 to	7 February 1959	*Earth Dog*
6 February 1970 to	26 January 1971	*Metal Dog*
25 January 1982 to	12 February 1983	*Water Dog*
10 February 1994 to	30 January 1995	*Wood Dog*

The Personality of the Dog

Firmness of purpose is one of the most necessary sinews of character, and one of the best instruments of success.
– *The Earl of Chesterfield: a Dog.*

The Dog is born under the signs of loyalty and anxiety. He usually holds very firm views and beliefs and is the champion of good causes. He hates any sort of injustice or unfair treatment and will do all in his power to help those less fortunate than himself. He has a strong sense of fair play and will be honourable and open in all his dealings.

The Dog is very direct and straightforward. He is never one to skirt round issues and speaks frankly and to the point. He can also be stubborn, but he is more than prepared to listen to the views of others and will try to be as fair as possible in coming to his decisions. He will readily give advice where it is needed and will be the first to offer assistance when things go wrong.

The Dog instils confidence wherever he goes and there are many who admire him for his integrity and resolute manner. He is a very good judge of character and he can often form an accurate impression of someone very shortly after meeting them. He is also very intuitive and can frequently sense how things are going to work out long in advance.

Despite his friendly and amiable manner, the Dog is not a big socializer. He dislikes having to attend large social functions or parties and much prefers a quiet meal with friends or a chat by the fire. The Dog is an excellent conversationalist and is often a marvellous raconteur of amusing stories and anecdotes.

He is also quick-witted and his mind is always alert. He can keep calm in a crisis and although he does have a temper, his outbursts tend to be short-lived. The Dog is loyal and trustworthy, but if he ever feels badly let down or rejected by someone, he will rarely forgive or forget.

The Dog usually has very set interests. He prefers to specialize and become an expert in a chosen area rather than dabble in a variety of different activities. He usually does well in jobs where he feels that he is being of service to others and is often suited to careers in the social services, the medical and legal professions and teaching. The Dog does, however, need to feel motivated in his work. He has to have a sense of purpose in the things that he does and if ever this is lacking he can quite often drift through life without ever achieving very much. Once he has the motivation, however, very little can prevent him from securing his objective.

Another characteristic of the Dog is his tendency to worry and to view things rather pessimistically. Quite often these worries are totally unnecessary and are of his own making. Although it may be difficult, worrying is a habit which the Dog should try to overcome.

The Dog is not materialistic or particularly bothered about accumulating great wealth. As long as he has the necessary money to support his family and to spend on the occasional luxury, he is more than happy. However, when he does have any spare money the Dog tends to be rather a spendthrift and does not always put his money to its best use. He is also not a very good speculator and would be advised to get professional advice before entering into any major long-term investment.

The Dog will rarely be short of admirers, but he is not an easy person to live with. His moods are changeable and his standards high, but he will be loyal and protective to his partner and will do all in his power to provide her with a good and comfortable home. He can get on extremely well with those born under the signs of the Horse, Pig, Tiger and Monkey, and can also establish a sound and stable relationship with the Rat, Ox, Rabbit, Snake and another Dog, but will find the Dragon a bit too flamboyant for his liking. He will also find it difficult to understand the creative and imaginative Goat and is likely to be highly irritated by the candid Rooster.

The female Dog is renowned for her beauty. She has a warm and caring nature, although until she knows someone well she can be both secretive and very guarded. She is highly intelligent and despite her calm and tranquil appearance she can be extremely ambitious. She enjoys sport and other outdoor activities and has a happy knack of finding bargains in the most unlikely of places. The female Dog can also get rather impatient when things do not work out as she would like.

The Dog usually has a very good way with children and can be a loving and doting parent.

The Dog will rarely be happier than when he is helping someone or doing something that will benefit others. Providing he can cure himself of his tendency to worry, he will lead a very full and active life – and in that life he will make many friends and do a tremendous amount of good.

The Five Different Types of Dog

In addition to the 12 signs of the Chinese zodiac, there are five elements and these have a strengthening or moderating influence on the sign. The effects of the five elements on the Dog are described below, together with the years in which the elements were exercising their influence. Therefore all Dogs born in 1910 and 1970 are Metal Dogs, those born in 1922 and 1982 are Water Dogs, and so on.

Metal Dog: 1910, 1970
The Metal Dog is bold, confident and forthright, and sets about everything he does in a resolute and determined manner. He has a great belief in his abilities and has no hesitation about speaking his mind or devoting himself to some just cause. He can be rather serious at times and can get anxious and irritable when things are not going according to plan. He tends to have very specific interests and it would certainly help him to broaden his outlook and also become more involved in group activities. He is extremely loyal and faithful to his friends.

Water Dog: 1922, 1982
The Water Dog has a very direct and outgoing personality. He is an excellent communicator and has little trouble in persuading others to fall in with his plans. He does, however, have a somewhat carefree nature and is not as disciplined or as thorough as he should be in certain matters. Neither does he keep as much control over his finances as he should, but he can be most generous to his family and friends and will make sure that they want for nothing. The Water Dog is usually very good with children and has a wide circle of friends.

Wood Dog: 1934, 1994
This Dog is a hard and conscientious worker and will usually make a favourable impression wherever he goes. He

is less independent than some of the other types of Dog and prefers to work in a group rather than on his own. He is popular, has a good sense of humour, and takes a very keen interest in the activities of the various members of his family. He is often attracted to the finer things in life and can get much pleasure from collecting stamps, coins, pictures or antiques. He also prefers to live in the country to the town.

Fire Dog: 1946
This Dog has a lively, outgoing personality and is able to establish friendships with remarkable ease. He is an honest and conscientious worker and likes to take an active part in all that is going on around him. He also likes to explore new ideas and, providing he can get the necessary support and advice, he can often succeed where others have failed. He does, however, have a tendency to be stubborn. Providing he can overcome this, the Fire Dog can often achieve considerable fame and fortune.

Earth Dog: 1898, 1958
The Earth Dog is very talented and astute. He is methodical and efficient and is capable of going far in his chosen profession. He tends to be rather quiet and reserved but has a very persuasive manner and usually secures his objectives without too much opposition. He is generous and kind and is always ready to lend a helping hand when it is needed. He is also held in very high esteem by his friends and colleagues and he is usually most dignified in his appearance.

Prospects for the Dog in 1994

The Chinese New Year starts on 10 February 1994. Until then, the old year, the Year of the Rooster, is still making its presence felt.

The Year of the Rooster (23 January 1993 to 9 February 1994) will have been a varied year for the Dog. Although he will have enjoyed some successes over the year, he will have found progress in certain areas difficult and disappointing. In some respects the Dog will have felt that he has been working hard but has little to show for his efforts. However, he should not be discouraged. The work he has undertaken and the experience he has gained will be an important contributory factor to the success he will enjoy in his own year, the Year of the Dog.

For what remains of the Rooster year, the Dog should persist in his various undertakings. In his work he should continue to give of his best and those Dogs seeking work should continue to pursue any opportunities that they see. By hard work and determination the Dog can and *will* make progress and he should not be discouraged by any set-backs that occur. The aspects are turning in his favour and he will notice these improved trends starting to appear in the closing stages of the Rooster year.

All this time the Dog should take careful note of what is going on around him and bear in mind the views of his family, friends and colleagues. This way he will not only be better informed about what is going on but will also be well placed to win their support. To remain independent or adopt a go-it-alone attitude, as some Dogs do, will only rebound on him and possibly leave him isolated when he does need support.

The Dog does need to exercise care in financial matters in the closing stages of the Rooster year. He should avoid taking risks with his money and it would also be in his interests to keep a watchful eye over his level of expenditure. The Dog should also try to deal with any outstanding correspondence or matters that he might have so that he will be freer and better placed to take advantage of the improved trends that await him in his own year.

The Year of the Dog starts on 10 February 1994 and is going to be an excellent year for the Dog. He can look forward to making great progress over the year and his achievements will amply compensate for any disappointments or set-backs that he may have experienced in recent years.

This is a year when the Dog can realize his own potential. He will find his ideas and plans will be well-received and that those around him will be supportive and co-operative. The Dog can achieve a great deal in 1994 and it rests with him to take advantage of the excellent trends that prevail.

In his work the Dog will make considerable progress. Others will readily recognize his abilities and talents and many Dogs will be promoted or move to a more rewarding position. The Dog should pursue any opportunities that he sees and if he has been thinking of changing his present type of work, this would be an excellent year to do so. For those seeking work, the prospects are certainly more favourable. By remaining determined and positive, their efforts will be rewarded – possibly when they least expect it. The Year of the Dog can often hold several pleasant surprises for the Dog and his career prospects are certainly favourably aspected in 1994.

Academic matters will also go well, and any Dog who has some spare time at his disposal would do well to consider learning a new skill or taking up a new interest. The year favours cultural pursuits and anything that the Dog can do to broaden his experience and skills will be time well spent.

The Dog will do well in financial matters and any Dog who may have had financial difficulties will find his situation eased during the year. For those Dogs who have spare funds at their disposal, 1994 is a good year for making investments, particularly any that would make provision for their long-term future. Most Dogs will, in any case, see a noticeable improvement in their financial situation over the year.

The Dog's family life will be generally settled and content and he can look forward to having some enjoyable times with those around him. He will find this a good year for joint activities and the Dog would do well to involve his family in his various activities. This is also a favourable year for carrying out home improvements or for moving and in either case the Dog will be pleased with how his plans work out.

The Dog's social life will be pleasant and he is likely to attend some most enjoyable social functions over the year as well as building up some new and meaningful friendships. Romance is especially well aspected and many Dogs who are unattached will meet their future partner in 1994 or get engaged or married. Those who are seeking new friends should make every effort to go out more and to attend events which would bring them in contact with others.

The travelling that the Dog undertakes in 1994 is likely to go well and he will enjoy any holidays or breaks he takes, particularly in the second half of the year.

Generally, 1994 is a highly favourable year for the Dog and he can do well in almost all his activities. However, his level of success is partly dependent on his own attitude and degree of determination. If he goes after specific objectives – whether it is a new job, a new home or some personal goal – he can reach them, but it does require action on his part. He would also do well to follow his intuition or any hunches that he has. In many instances, his own feelings will prove uncannily accurate and if he has a major decision to make over the year, he should take careful note of his own intuition.

Any problems that the Dog encounters this year are likely to be relatively small and can be quickly dealt with. However, the main danger to the Dog in 1994 is inaction. If he is prepared to drift through the year without going after any objectives, or is prepared to rest content with past and present achievements, he could miss some excellent opportunities. This is a year for being bold, positive and determined and for the Dog who is prepared to act, take chances and go after his objectives, the rewards of the year can be great indeed.

As far as the different types of Dog are concerned, 1994 will be both a challenging and highly rewarding year for the **Metal Dog**. Over the year several important changes will take place and out of these will come new and brighter opportunities. These changes could involve the Metal Dog moving to another area or taking a new job. In either case, the changes will present challenges, but with determination and his usual strong will the Metal Dog will emerge from the year with some worthy gains to his credit. Throughout the year he should pursue any openings that he sees and try to broaden his skills and experience. He should also not be discouraged by any set-backs that occur but should regard them as challenges to overcome, to learn from and to triumph over. By remaining positive and determined, 1994 can be a truly successful year for him. He will also be fortunate in financial matters, although he should still be wary of stretching his resources too far. On a personal level, this will be a memorable year and many Metal Dogs will have good cause for a personal celebration – either by getting engaged, married or seeing an addition to their families. Socially, the Metal Dog will be much in demand and his circle of acquaintances will increase quite substantially. He will also receive much valuable support from others over the year and it would be in his interests to tell others of his plans, his hopes and aspirations for the future. By being open in this way, those around him will be better placed to help him and this will be very much to his advantage. The Year of the Dog is going to be a significant year for the Metal Dog and he should make every effort to pursue his aims and objectives as far as he can. For the determined Metal Dog, this can be a most auspicious year!

The **Water Dog** will enjoy 1994. If, in recent years, he has been lonely or had some difficulties to overcome, he should regard this as a year of rejuvenation and of new opportunities. He should make every effort to go out more, take up new interests and act in a positive manner. Socially, this can be a busy and eventful year and will hold many happy moments for him. His circle of friends will increase, any travelling that he undertakes will go well and his various interests will give him much satisfaction. He will also be able to delight in the achievements of a close relation and this will be a great source of pride to him. The Water Dog will, however, have to make several important decisions over the year and these will have a bearing on his long-term future. In making these decisions, he would do well to bear in mind the views of the members of his family and his close friends. He will be greatly reassured by the advice he is given and, while he may not like to trouble others with any worries or uncertainties that he has, he will find much truth in the saying 'A problem shared is a problem halved.' Those Water Dogs involved in education will also make important progress and some new skills that they are able to obtain will prove of great value in years to come. Generally, 1994 will be a good and rewarding year for the Water Dog and by adopting a positive outlook, he will not only enjoy the year but be pleased with how events work out for him.

This will be a memorable and eventful year for the **Wood Dog**. However, to get the best from the year he should have some idea of what he would like to achieve over the year and what he would like to do with his time. Without any plan or objective he could easily miss out on some good opportunities and not make the best use of his skills and talents. Also, if he does have any spare time at his disposal, he should aim to fill that time constructively. It is an ideal year for the Wood Dog to take up a new interest or undertake home improvements – he will find either or both most satisfying. He will also greatly enjoy any travelling that he undertakes and it would be a good time for him to visit places that he has wanted to see for some time or to visit distant relations. The Wood Dog will be fortunate in financial matters in 1994 and many can look forward to receiving an additional sum of money over the year. Socially and domestically, this will be a pleasant year for the Wood Dog and he will have some most enjoyable times with his family and friends. Generally, 1994 is a favourable year for him but the amount he accomplishes does rest with him. By acting positively and constructively he can do well and will enjoy the year. March, August and October are likely to be particularly pleasing months for him.

The **Fire Dog** will see a considerable improvement in his fortunes in 1994. If he has not been making the progress that he would have liked or has had some difficulties to contend with over the last few years, this will be the year in which he can put past disappointments and set-backs behind him and make new progress. He will have learnt much from the experiences of recent years and this he can put to good use. The Fire Dog is likely to do well in his work and if he is seeking a job or promotion or wanting to change his career he should pursue any opportunities that he sees. All Fire Dogs would do well to try and add to their skills over the year and if the Fire Dog is able to go on any training courses he will find that this will do much to enhance his future prospects. In 1994 he needs to act positively and resolutely and be determined to make the most of his considerable talents. The rewards of his labours can be great and it is up to him to take advantage of the positive trends that prevail. He will also see an improvement in his financial position, although he could be involved in several expensive undertakings over the year, particularly if he moves or has any home improvements carried out. In either case it would be in his interests to obtain as many quotations as possible and also check the terms of any financial undertaking he is about to enter. The Fire Dog will be much in demand with his family and friends over the year and will lead a generally pleasant domestic and social life.

This will be a positive and fulfilling year for the **Earth Dog**. Over the year he will make considerable progress in many of his activities. However, to obtain the best results in 1994 the Earth Dog should have some clear idea of what he wants to achieve and then work purposefully towards that objective. Without some plan or goal he could miss some ideal opportunities and achieve less satisfying results. This particularly applies in his work. If a new job, promotion or a change of career is his aim, all are possible but the Earth Dog must first be sure in his mind what it is he wants and then go after his goal. By remaining determined and aware of all that is going on around him, he can make excellent progress. He will also be helped by the support and encouragement that his family and friends are able to give. Domestically, this will be a most pleasant year for him and the Earth Dog is likely to take particular delight in the achievements and success of someone close to him. His social life will also be enjoyable and over the course of the year the Earth Dog is likely to build up some new friends. These could prove of great value to him in future years. The Earth Dog will be successful in financial matters and if he is able to put any spare money he has into a long-term savings policy, he could find that this will build into a worthwhile asset in years to come. Generally, 1994 will be a very good year for the Earth Dog and the aspects are favourable in almost all areas of his life. It rests with him to decide what it is he wants to achieve over the year and then follow that aim. Luck and good fortune are on his side.

Famous Dogs

André Agassi, Kingsley Amis, Jane Asher, Kenneth Baker, Brigitte Bardot, Dr Christiaan Barnard, Candice Bergman, Lionel Blair, Simon le Bon, Betty Boo, Dr Boutros-Ghali, David Bowie, Peter Brooke, Kate Bush, Max Bygraves, King Carl Gustaf XVI of Sweden, Belinda Carlisle, Paul Cézanne, Cher, Sir Winston Churchill, Petula Clark, Bill Clinton, Leonard Cohen, Robin Cook, Henry Cooper, Edwina

Currie, Jamie Lee Curtis, Timothy Dalton, Charles Dance, Christopher Dean, Claude Debussy, John Dunn, Blake Edwards, Sally Field, Zsa Zsa Gabor, Judy Garland, Bamber Gascoigne, George Gershwin, Lenny Henry, Patricia Hodge, Frankie Howerd, Victor Hugo, Barry Humphries, Michael Jackson, Henry Kelly, Felicity Kendal, Nik Kershaw, Sue Lawley, Maureen Lipman, Sophia Loren, Joanna Lumley, Shirley MacLaine, Madonna, Norman Mailer, Barry Manilow, Rik Mayall, Simon Mayo, Golda Meir, Freddie Mercury, Liza Minnelli, David Niven, Gary Numan, Sydney Pollack, Elvis Presley, Anneka Rice, Malcolm Rifkind, Paul Robeson, Linda Ronstadt, Gabriela Sabatini, Carl Sagan, Jennifer Saunders, Norman Schwarzkopf, Sylvester Stallone, Robert Louis Stevenson, David Suchet, Donald Sutherland, Mother Teresa, Voltaire, Timothy West, Mary Whitehouse, Prince William, Ian Woosnam.

The Pig

30 January 1911 to	17 February 1912	***Metal Pig***
16 February 1923 to	4 February 1924	***Water Pig***
4 February 1935 to	23 January 1936	***Wood Pig***
22 January 1947 to	9 February 1948	***Fire Pig***
8 February 1959 to	27 January 1960	***Earth Pig***
27 January 1971 to	14 February 1972	***Metal Pig***
13 February 1983 to	1 February 1984	***Water Pig***

The Personality of the Pig

Enthusiasm is the yeast that makes your hopes rise to the stars. Enthusiasm is the sparkle in your eyes, the swing in your gait, the grip of your hand, the irresistible surge of will and energy to execute your ideas.

– *Henry Ford: a Pig.*

The Pig is born under the sign of honesty. He has a kind and understanding nature and is well-known for his abilities as a peace-maker. He hates any sort of discord or unpleasantness and will do all in his power to sort out differences of opinion or bring opposing factions together.

He is an excellent conversationalist and speaks truthfully and to the point. He dislikes any form of falsehood or hypocrisy and is a firm believer in justice and the maintenance of law and order. In spite of these beliefs, however, the Pig is reasonably tolerant and often prepared to forgive others for their wrongs. The Pig rarely harbours grudges and is never vindictive.

The Pig is usually very popular. He enjoys other people's company and likes to be involved in joint or group activities. He will be a loyal member of any club or society and can be relied upon to lend a helping hand at functions. He is also an excellent fund-raiser for charities and is often a great supporter of humanitarian causes.

The Pig is a hard and conscientious worker and is particularly respected for his reliability and integrity. In his early years he will try his hand at several different jobs, but he is usually happiest where he feels that he is being of service to others. He will unselfishly give up his time for the common good and is highly-valued by his colleagues and employers.

The Pig has a good sense of humour and invariably has a smile, joke or some whimsical remark at the ready. He loves to entertain and to please others, and there are many who have been attracted to careers in show business or who enjoy following the careers of famous stars and personalities.

There are, unfortunately, some who take advantage of the Pig's good nature and impose on his generosity. The Pig has great difficulty in saying 'no' and, although he may dislike being firm, it would be in his own interests to say occasionally, 'Enough is enough.' The Pig can also be rather naïve and gullible; if at any stage in his life he feels that he has been badly let down, he will make sure that it will never happen again and will try to become self-reliant. There are many Pigs who have become entrepreneurs or forged a successful career on their own after some early disappointment in life. And although the Pig tends to spend his money quite freely, he is usually very astute in financial matters and there are many Pigs who have become wealthy.

Another characteristic of the Pig is his ability to recover from set-backs reasonably quickly. His faith and his strength of character keep him going. If he thinks that there is a job he can do – or has something that he wants to achieve – he will pursue it with a dogged determination. He can also be stubborn and, no matter how many may plead with him, once he has made his mind up he will rarely change his views.

Although the Pig may work hard, he also knows how to enjoy himself. He is a great pleasure-seeker and will quite happily spend his hard-earned money on a lavish holiday or an expensive meal – for the Pig is a connoisseur of good food and wine – or take part in a variety of recreational activities. He also enjoys small social gatherings and, if he is in company he likes, the Pig can very easily become the life and soul of the party. He does, however, tend to become rather withdrawn at larger functions or when among strangers.

The Pig is also a creature of comfort and his home will usually be fitted with all the latest in luxury appliances. Where possible, he will prefer to live in the country to the town and will opt to have a big garden, for the Pig is usually a keen and successful gardener.

The Pig is very popular with the opposite sex and will often have numerous romances before he settles down. Once settled, however, he will be loyal and protective to his partner and he will find that he is especially well-suited to those born under the signs of the Goat, Rabbit, Dog and Tiger, and also to another Pig. Due to his affable and easy-going nature he can also establish a satisfactory relationship with all the remaining signs of the Chinese zodiac, with the exception of the Snake. The Snake tends to be wily, secretive and very guarded, and this can be intensely irritating to the honest and open-hearted Pig.

The lady Pig will devote all her energies to the needs of her children and her partner. She will try to ensure that they want for nothing and their pleasure is very much her pleasure. Her home will either be very clean and orderly or hopelessly untidy. Strangely, there seems to be no in between with the Pig – they either love housework or detest it! The lady Pig does, however, have considerable talents as an organizer and this, combined with her friendly and open manner, enables her to secure many of her objectives. She can also be a caring and conscientious parent and has very good taste in clothes.

The Pig is usually lucky in life and will rarely want for anything. Provided he does not let others take advantage of his good nature and is not afraid of asserting himself, he will go through life making friends, helping others and winning the admiration of many.

The Five Different Types of Pig

In addition to the 12 signs of the Chinese zodiac, there are five elements and these have a strengthening or moderating influence on the sign. The effects of the five elements on the Pig are described below, together with the years in which the elements were exercising their influence. Therefore all Pigs born in 1911 and 1971 are Metal Pigs, those born in 1923 and 1983 are Water Pigs, and so on.

Metal Pig: 1911, 1971
The Metal Pig is more ambitious and determined than some of the other types of Pig. He is strong, energetic and likes to be involved in a wide variety of different activities. He is very open and forthright in his views, although he can be a little too trusting at times and has a tendency to accept things at face value. He has a good sense of humour and loves to attend parties and other social gatherings. He has a warm, outgoing nature and usually has a large circle of friends.

Water Pig: 1923, 1983
The Water Pig has a heart of gold. He is generous and loyal and tries to remain on good terms with everyone. He will do his utmost to help others, but sadly there are some who

will take advantage of his kind nature and he should, in his own interests, be a little more discriminating and be prepared to stand firm against anything that he does not like. Although he prefers the quieter things in life, he has a wide range of interests. He particularly enjoys outdoor pursuits and attending parties and social occasions. He is a hard and conscientious worker and invariably does well in his chosen profession. He is also gifted in the art of communication.

Wood Pig: 1935
This Pig has a friendly, persuasive manner and is easily able to gain the confidence of others. He likes to be involved in all that is going on around him and can sometimes take on more responsibility than he can properly handle. He is loyal to his family and friends and he also derives much pleasure from helping those less fortunate than himself. The Wood Pig is usually an optimist and leads a very full, enjoyable and satisfying life. He also has a good sense of humour.

Fire Pig: 1947
The Fire Pig is both energetic and adventurous and he sets about everything he does in a confident and resolute manner. He is very forthright in his views and does not mind taking risks in order to achieve his objectives. He can, however, get carried away by the excitement of the moment and ought to exercise more caution with some of the enterprises in which he gets involved. The Fire Pig is usually lucky in money matters and is well known for his generosity. He is also very caring towards the members of his family.

Earth Pig: 1899, 1959
This Pig has a kindly nature. He is sensible and realistic and will go to great lengths in order to please his employers and to secure his aims and ambitions. He is an excellent organizer and is particularly astute in business and financial

matters. He has a good sense of humour and a wide circle of friends. He also likes to lead an active social life, although he does sometimes have a tendency to eat and drink more than is good for him.

Prospects for the Pig in 1994

The Chinese New Year starts on 10 February 1994. Until then, the old year, the Year of the Rooster, is still making its presence felt.

The Year of the Rooster (23 January 1993 to 9 February 1994) will have been a busy and generally fulfilling year for the Pig. Over the year there will have been many demands on his time and, while he may not have achieved all that he would have liked, his results and progress will have generally been satisfying. The Pig is likely to have done well in his work, particularly in to the latter part of the Rooster year.

For what remains of this Chinese year, the Pig should remain alert for opportunities to pursue and to promote his talents and skills as much as he can. Career prospects for the Pig are well aspected in the Rooster year and he should make the most of the favourable trends that prevail, especially in October and November 1993 and January 1994. At this time he will find much truth in the saying, 'Nothing ventured, nothing gained.'

Financial matters will also go well and should the Pig have any spare money in the Rooster year, he should consider saving or investing it rather than spending it on items that he may not really want. Sometimes the Pig can be rather too indulgent for his own good, and it would be in his interests to be a little more restrained in his spending, especially in the latter half of the Rooster year.

Domestically and socially, the Rooster year is a pleasant time for the Pig and in the closing stages of the year he will find himself much in demand. He will enjoy several social functions and can also look forward to receiving some good and rather unexpected news concerning a close relation or friend.

Although the latter part of the Rooster year will be a busy time for the Pig, he should make sure that he sets some time aside for recreational activities and gives himself the opportunity to rest and unwind. If he has an interest or hobby he can turn to, he is likely to find this both satisfying and beneficial. If he does not have such an interest, it would be worthwhile taking one up. The Rooster year is a constructive year for the Pig and anything that he can do to further his interests, his skills or his career will be of lasting benefit to him.

The Year of the Dog begins on 10 February 1994 and is going to be a varied and interesting year for the Pig. He will be able to consolidate any gains he has made over the last 12 months, but more significantly he will be able to lay the foundation for the super progress he will make in his own year, 1995, the Year of the Pig. So the Year of the Dog is a year for gaining experience and for planning for the future. During the year all Pigs should carefully analyse their present position and think about any changes they would like to take place or objectives they would like to reach. Then, with some plan in mind, the Pig should look for ways in which he can bring about these changes. By planning in this way and taking stock of his present position, he will feel more motivated to take steps to bring about positive changes and developments in his life. In this respect 1994 is an important year and the work which the Pig accomplishes and the plans he draws up are likely to have a significant bearing on his progress in the next few years.

Throughout 1994 the Pig will make pleasing progress in his work. Many Pigs will be given new responsibilities or obtain a different position and, despite any initial misgivings they may have, these changes will work out well for them. However, in his work the Pig should be wary of taking the support of others for granted or of setting himself unrealistic objectives. Progress is likely, but it will be modest rather than dramatic. Pigs seeking work should remain alert for opportunities to pursue and should also investigate types of work which they might not have considered before. They could find a different type of work more stimulating and challenging as well as leading to greater opportunities in the future.

The Pig would also do well to consider adding to his skills over the year – perhaps by enrolling on a course or taking up a new interest. Culturally and academically, this is a most favourable year for him and anything that he can do to enhance his prospects will be time well spent, especially with the excellent opportunities for advancement that await him in 1995.

Financially, this will also be a good year and many Pigs can look forward to seeing an improvement in their financial situation over the year. The Pig will be generally fortunate in any investments that he makes, but at the same time he should be wary of any particularly risky or speculative ventures that he hears about. Provided they are careful and conservative, almost all Pigs will end the year in a stronger financial position than at the start.

The Pig can look forward to having some pleasant times with his family and friends in 1994, and domestically many Pigs will obtain considerable satisfaction by spending time on DIY projects or carrying out improvements around the home.

The Pig may also have to assist a close relation who has a difficult problem to overcome and his patience, sincerity and sensible advice will be much appreciated.

The Pig should ensure that he regularly sets some time aside for relaxation and recreation this year. Despite his good intentions, he does tend to drive himself very hard and put himself under considerable pressure. Over the year he should make sure that he does not neglect his own well-being and, if possible, he should try to take some short breaks at different times of the year. He is likely to find these most beneficial for him.

Although this will be a generally favourable year for the Pig, there are several points that he would do well to consider. If he meets with any set-backs or finds himself criticized for any endeavour, he should look closely at the reasons why. By taking a constructive attitude, the Pig will be able to learn and benefit from any mistakes he may have made in the past. He should also make sure that he has the backing and support of others before embarking on any new undertaking. Although his relations with others will generally go well, at no time during the year can the Pig afford to act independently.

The Pig will, however, be blessed with a certain amount of luck in 1994, particularly in the closing months of the year. He would do well to enter any competitions that interest him and also follow up any tempting opportunities that he sees. The year is likely to contain some unexpected surprises for the Pig!

Generally, 1994 will be a pleasant and favourable year for the Pig. He can make a reasonable amount of progress in many of his activities, but his biggest gains are likely to come from the plans he makes and the experience that he obtains over the year. The Year of the Dog is a year for the Pig to gain experience, to plan and prepare himself for the considerable advances that await him in 1995, his own year, the Year of the Pig.

As far as the different types of Pig are concerned, 1994 will be an important and constructive year for the **Metal Pig**. He will make steady progress in his career and towards the latter part of the year several new openings and opportunities will present themselves which he would do well to follow up. He should also take any opportunity that he has to add to his skills. He will find that his accomplishments and the experience he gains over the year will contribute to the considerable progress that he will make in the next few years. However, in all his activities, he should avoid taking unnecessary risks and, as far as possible, try to spread his activities out over the year. To try to rush things or accomplish a lot in a short time will only put him under a lot of pressure as well as leading to less satisfying results. In 1994, time is on his side and he would do well to bear in mind the Chinese proverb, 'A little impatience spoils great plans.' Personally, this will be a happy and memorable year for him and many Metal Pigs will have good cause for a celebration over the year, including perhaps an addition to the family. The Metal Pig will also be successful in financial matters, but when dealing with finance, he does need to check the terms of any important agreement he is about to enter very carefully and, if he is unsure about the meaning of any part of the agreement, he should seek advice. As with most things in 1994, to take risks could cause problems, but providing he is careful and cautious he will do well. The Metal Pig will enjoy any travelling that he undertakes in 1994 and a holiday taken in the late summer could prove particularly enjoyable for him. Generally, the Metal Pig will enjoy 1994 but during the year he would do well to give some thought to his future and to what he would like to achieve over the next few years.

This will be a quiet and pleasant year for the **Water Pig**. Over the year he will be able to devote time to his family and his own interests and both are likely to give him much pleasure and satisfaction. Domestic matters will generally go well and those around him will be supportive and co-operative regarding his plans and ideas. However, if there is any matter troubling him, the Water Pig should not hesitate to seek the views of others. To keep any problem to himself will only increase the worry and in the end he could even find out that he is worrying himself unnecessarily. The Water Pig can also look forward to attending some important social functions over the year, and if he has been feeling lonely in recent years, he would do well to go out more and to meet and get in contact with others. If he does, he will be glad he made the effort. All Water Pigs will build up some good and long-lasting friendships over the year. The Water Pig will be fortunate in financial matters and could be lucky in a competition that he enters. The year also favours cultural and creative pursuits and the Water Pig would do well to set some time aside for any activities that interest him. He will find that these will give him much satisfaction as well as being a valuable source of relaxation. Those Water Pigs in education are likely to do well and make good progress over the year.

This will be a pleasant year for the **Wood Pig** and he can look forward to making progress in many of his activities. His family life will be content and settled and he will have some happy and memorable times with those around him. His social life will also be most enjoyable and many Wood Pigs will find that their circle of friends and acquaintances will widen appreciably over the year. If the Wood Pig has been thinking of moving, this would be a good year to do so or to look at areas where he might like to live. The Wood Pig will be fortunate in financial matters and by looking around he could buy some items for himself and for his home at most advantageous prices. While this will be a generally good year for him, he would do well to give some thought to his future and to what he would like to accomplish in the next few years. The latter part of the Dog year and the Year of the Pig will be a most significant time for him and in order to take advantage of the trends that prevail, he should be sure in his mind of what he would like to achieve. Much of 1994 should be regarded as a time to plan for the future. Towards the end of the year and throughout 1995 will be the time to put these plans into practice. The Wood Pig will also be helped by discussing his ideas with those around him and he will be pleased with how well his views and ideas are received. One area which he should watch over the year, however, is attending to detailed correspondence. It would be in his interests to deal with any important forms carefully, as a mistake could be to his detriment and take some time to sort out.

This will be an interesting but challenging year for the **Fire Pig**. Most of his activities will work out in his favour but he may have a few minor problems to overcome. Although these could cause him some annoyance at the time, the Fire Pig should not allow himself to become disheartened or, in the case of any set-backs, too resentful. The events of the year will help to lay the foundations for the greater progress he will make in the next few years. Also, by rethinking some of his plans and focusing his attention on his present situation, he will be able to get a better idea of his true objectives and what it is he really wants to achieve. In this respect, irrespective of any problems or set-backs that occur, 1994 will be an important and significant year and will serve as a prelude to the better times ahead. In his career, the Fire Pig is likely to make constructive progress, particularly in the latter part of the year. If, however, he is looking for work or is unhappy in his present position he would do well to pursue any opportunities that he sees and also investigate types of work which he may not have fully considered before. He has many different talents and over the year he will be able to put some of these to good use. The Fire Pig can look forward to having some most pleasant times with his family and many will have good cause for a family celebration over the year. The Fire Pig will also do well in financial matters and could see a noticeable improvement in his financial situation towards the end of the year. Generally, this will be a pleasing year for him and providing he sets about his activities in his usual conscientious manner, he will make useful progress as well as sowing the seeds for the even greater progress he will make in 1995.

This will be a pleasing year for the **Earth Pig**. He can look forward to having some splendid times with his family and friends and he will be particularly proud of the achievements of someone very close to him. The support and encouragement he is able to give will prove of considerable value. The Earth Pig's social life is likely to be busier than in recent years and during 1994 he will establish many new contacts and friends. Some of these could be particularly helpful to him in the future. Indeed, throughout the year the Earth Pig would do well to watch and listen to all that is going on around him as he could pick up some ideas or information which will be useful to him later. He will make progress in his work over the year and many Earth Pigs will be successful in obtaining a new position or be given additional responsibilities. There will, however, be occasions over the year when the Earth Pig will have many demands on his time and on these occasions he should not hesitate to ask others for assistance. It would also be helpful for him to set himself priorities for the year rather than squandering his energies on trying to undertake too much all at the same time. Also, in view of the many demands on his time, it is important that he does set some regular time aside for recreational pursuits. He could find some suitable sporting or outdoor activity particularly beneficial for him. The Earth Pig will be generally fortunate in financial matters and October and November are likely to be two important and auspicious months for him.

Famous Pigs

Russ Abbot, Bryan Adams, Woody Allen, Julie Andrews, Fred Astaire, Sir Richard Attenborough, Simon Bates, Jeremy Beadle, Gerhard Berger, Hector Berlioz, David Blunkett, Humphrey Bogart, Maria Callas, Dr George Carey, Richard Chamberlain, Glen Close, Brian Clough, Sir Noël Coward, Oliver Cromwell, the Dalai Lama, Sir Robin Day, Lord Denning, Richard Dreyfuss, Sheena Easton, Ralph Waldo Emerson, David Essex, Farrah Fawcett, Henry Ford, Debbie Greenwood, Emmylou Harris, Chesney Hawkes,

William Randolph Hearst, Ernest Hemingway, Henry VIII, Alfred Hitchcock, King Hussein of Jordan, Elton John, C.G. Jung, Boris Karloff, Stephen King, Henry Kissinger, Jerry Lee Lewis, John McEnroe, Marcel Marceau, Ngaio Marsh, Johnny Mathis, Montgomery of Alamein, Dudley Moore, Patrick Moore, John Mortimer, Wolfgang Amadeus Mozart, Michael Parkinson, Luciano Pavarotti, Lester Piggott, Maurice Ravel, Dan Quayle, Ronald Reagan, Albert Reynolds, John D. Rockefeller, Ginger Rogers, Nick Ross, Sade, Salman Rushdie, Baroness Sue Ryder of Warsaw, Pete Sampras, Arantxa Sanchez, Telly Savalas, Arnold Schwarzenegger, Albert Schweitzer, Donald Sinden, Steven Spielberg, Tracey Ullman, the Duchess of York.

Appendix

The relationship between the 12 animal signs – both on a personal level and business level – is an important aspect of Chinese horoscopes and in this Appendix the compatibility between the signs is shown in the two tables that follow. Also included are the names of the signs ruling the hours of the day and from this it is possible to find your ascendant and discover yet another aspect of your personality.

Personal Relationships

Key
1 Excellent. Great rapport.
2 A successful relationship. Many interests in common.
3 Mutual respect and understanding. A good relationship.
4 Fair. Needs care and some willingness to compromise in order for the relationship to work.
5 Awkward. Possible difficulties in communication with few interests in common.
6 A clash of personalities. Very difficult.

	Rat	Ox	Tiger	Rabbit	Dragon	Snake	Horse	Goat	Monkey	Rooster	Dog	Pig
Rat	1											
Ox	1	3										
Tiger	4	6	5									
Rabbit	5	2	3	3								
Dragon	1	5	5	3	2							
Snake	3	1	6	2	1	5						
Horse	6	5	1	4	3	4	2					
Goat	5	5	3	1	4	3	2	2				
Monkey	1	3	6	3	1	3	5	3	1			
Rooster	4	1	4	6	2	1	2	4	5	5		
Dog	3	4	1	3	6	3	2	5	3	5	2	
Pig	2	3	2	2	3	6	3	2	2	3	1	2

APPENDIX

Business Relationships

Key
1 Excellent. Marvellous understanding and rapport.
2 Very good. Complement each other well.
3 A good working relationship and understanding can be developed.
4 Fair, but compromise and a common objective is often needed to make this relationship work.
5 Awkward. Unlikely to work, either through lack of trust, understanding or the competitiveness of the signs.
6 Mistrust. Difficult. To be avoided.

	Rat	Ox	Tiger	Rabbit	Dragon	Snake	Horse	Goat	Monkey	Rooster	Dog	Pig
Rat	2											
Ox	1	3										
Tiger	3	6	5									
Rabbit	4	3	4	3								
Dragon	1	4	3	4	3							
Snake	3	2	6	4	1	5						
Horse	6	4	1	4	3	4	3					
Goat	4	5	3	1	4	3	3	2				
Monkey	2	3	4	5	1	5	4	4	3			
Rooster	5	1	5	5	2	1	2	5	4	6		
Dog	4	5	2	3	6	3	2	5	3	5	3	
Pig	3	3	2	2	4	5	4	2	3	4	3	3

Your Ascendant

The ascendant has a very strong influence on your personality and, together with the information already given about your sign and the effects of the element on your sign, it will help you gain even greater insight into your true personality according to Chinese horoscopes.

The hours of the day are named after the 12 animal signs and the sign governing the time you were born is your ascendant. To find your ascendant, look up the time of your birth on the table below, bearing in mind any local time differences in the place you were born.

11 p.m. to 1 a.m.	The hours of the Rat
1 a.m. to 3 a.m.	The hours of the Ox
3 a.m. to 5 a.m.	The hours of the Tiger
5 a.m. to 7 a.m.	The hours of the Rabbit
7 a.m. to 9 a.m.	The hours of the Dragon
9 a.m. to 11 a.m.	The hours of the Snake
11 a.m. to 1 p.m.	The hours of the Horse
1 p.m. to 3 p.m.	The hours of the Goat
3 p.m. to 5 p.m.	The hours of the Monkey
5 p.m. to 7 p.m.	The hours of the Rooster
7 p.m. to 9 p.m.	The hours of the Dog
9 p.m. to 11 p.m.	The hours of the Pig

Rat: The influence of the Rat as ascendant is likely to make the sign more outgoing, sociable and also more careful with money. A particularly beneficial influence for those born under the sign of the Rabbit, Horse, Monkey and Pig.

Ox: The Ox as ascendant has a restraining, cautionary and steadying influence which many signs will benefit from. This ascendant also promotes self-confidence and will-power and is an especially good ascendant for those born under the signs of the Tiger, Rabbit and Goat.

Tiger: This ascendant is a dynamic and stirring influence which makes the sign more outgoing, more action-orientated and more impulsive. A generally favourable ascendant for the Ox, Tiger, Snake and Horse.

Rabbit: The Rabbit as ascendant has a moderating influence, making the sign more reflective, serene and discreet. A particularly beneficial influence for the Rat, Dragon, Monkey and Rooster.

Dragon: The Dragon as ascendant gives strength, determination and an added ambition to the sign. A favourable influence for those born under the signs of the Rabbit, Goat, Monkey and Dog.

Snake: The Snake as ascendant can make the sign more reflective, more intuitive and more self-reliant. A good influence for the Tiger, Goat and Pig.

Horse: The influence of the Horse will make the sign more adventurous, more daring and, on some occasions, more fickle. Generally a beneficial influence for the Rabbit, Snake, Dog and Pig.

Goat: This ascendant will make the sign more tolerant, easy-going and receptive. The Goat could also impart some creative and artistic qualities to the sign. An especially good influence for the Ox, Dragon, Snake and Rooster.

Monkey: The Monkey as ascendant is likely to impart a delicious sense of humour and fun to the sign. He will make the sign more enterprising and outgoing – a particularly good influence for the Rat, Ox, Snake and Goat.

Rooster: The Rooster as ascendant helps to give the sign a lively, outgoing and very methodical manner. Its influence will increase efficiency and is a good influence for the Ox, Tiger, Rabbit and Horse.

Dog: The Dog as ascendant makes the sign more reasonable and fair-minded as well as giving an added sense of loyalty. A very good ascendant for the Tiger, Dragon and Goat.

Pig: The influence of the Pig can make the sign more sociable, content and self-indulgent. It is also a caring influence and one which can make the sign want to help others. A good ascendant for the Dragon and Monkey.

How to Get the Best from the Year

One of the chief values of Chinese horoscopes is that they help to identify trends for the forthcoming year. Once these trends have been identified, it is possible for each sign to know what areas of life are likely to proceed well and which could prove more troublesome. With this knowledge, the more favourably aspected areas can be concentrated on and care can be taken in those areas where the aspects are not so favourable. In this respect, Chinese horoscopes can serve as a useful guide.

Here, to supplement the earlier sections on the prospects

for each of the signs, I have indicated how I believe each of the signs will fare in 1994 and how each can get the best from the year. The areas covered are: general prospects, finance, career prospects and relations with others.

General Prospects

Rat: A reasonably good year, but the Rat should try to set himself some objectives and priorities for the year. The best results will come from concentrating on areas that are familiar to him rather than attempting anything new or too ambitious.

Ox: The Ox is blessed with a very determined nature and this will certainly help in the Year of the Dog. Small problems could emerge and the Ox could experience some setbacks, but by persevering he will be able to ride out any difficulties that arise and end the year with gains to his credit.

Tiger: A good year ahead. However, to do well the Tiger should concentrate on specific objectives and if new circumstances arise, be flexible in his outlook. The Tiger should also not be afraid of taking up new challenges – either by taking up a different sort of work or new interests. He will find the challenge this will offer stimulating as well as leading to new and brighter opportunities.

Rabbit: A reasonably good year. To get the best results, the Rabbit should decide upon his objectives and work purposefully towards attaining them. Determination will bring positive results.

Dragon: A variable year ahead. However, if the Dragon sets about his activities with care and can keep his rather impulsive nature in check, his prospects for the year will not be too bad and he will be able to make a reasonable amount of progress. This is, however, not a year for hasty action, for taking risks or pushing his Dragon luck too far!

Snake: A generally favourable year. However, the Snake does need to be positive over the year and remain firmly committed to his aims and aspirations. To weaken his resolve, become distracted or just be content with past achievements will mean that he misses out on some excellent opportunities and does not make the most of his considerable talents. A year to be bold and determined. Travel is also well aspected.

Horse: An exciting year ahead. Many opportunities await the Horse in 1994 and throughout the year he would do well to act boldly and with determination. Over the year, the Horse will see many changes taking place and out of these changes will come new and interesting opportunities, which the Horse can turn to his advantage.

Goat: Although not the best of years for the Goat, 1994 will provide valuable opportunities. By being realistic in his objectives and taking any opportunity to add to his skills and experience, the Goat can pave the way for future successes. This is a year for learning, planning and preparation, with the rewards coming through in 1995 and 1996.

APPENDIX

Monkey: A reasonable year ahead, although the Monkey does need to exercise care in his various activities. To achieve the best results, he needs to plan and proceed cautiously. This is not a year for embarking on ambitious new projects or for taking unnecessary risks.

Rooster: Although the Rooster may have a few obstacles to overcome in 1994, this need not offset the steady progress he can make. He should set about his activities in his usual methodical way and will find that the best results can be obtained by concentrating on areas that are familiar to him rather than experimenting with new activities.

Dog: A most favourable year ahead. The Dog should regard 1994 as a year of new opportunities, a year to build on his experience and a time to put past set-backs behind him. With determination and a positive outlook, this can be a most fulfilling, enjoyable and successful year for him.

Pig: A pleasant and constructive year ahead. The Pig should continue to set about his activities in his usual conscientious manner, but he would do well to try and increase his skills and experience over the year and also give some thought to his future. This is a year for learning and for planning, with the results of his labours coming through late in 1994 and in 1995.

Finance

Rat: Although not a bad year financially, the Rat should keep a careful watch over his outgoings and avoid being too extravagant in his spending. Money he is able to save could prove useful later in the year.

Ox: Financial matters will go reasonably well, although the Ox would do well not to stretch his resources too far.

Tiger: A favourable year for money matters. The Tiger can, however, sometimes be rather extravagant in his spending and in 1994 it would be in his interests to try and save some money. If he takes out a savings policy now, he could find this is a valuable asset in years to come.

Rabbit: The Rabbit will see a steady improvement in his financial position over the year, although it would be in his interests to keep a close watch over his general level of outgoings.

Dragon: Care is needed. Not a year for taking risks, getting involved in speculative ventures or for being too extravagant.

Snake: A fortunate year for financial matters, provided the Snake stays clear of risky ventures and does not gamble!

Horse: A generally favourable year for financial matters. Many Horses will see an improvement in their financial position over the year.

Goat: Care is needed. This is not a year for taking risks or for being too extravagant.

Monkey: This is not a year for taking risks or becoming involved in speculative ventures. In 1994 the Monkey needs to be prudent and avoid stretching his resources too far.

Rooster: A year to be careful in all financial matters.

Dog: Although the Dog could be involved in several large financial undertakings over the year, particularly if he moves or has home improvements carried out, financial matters will go well. It would, however, be in his interests to keep a watchful eye on his general outgoings and check all the details and implications very carefully before entering into any large financial transaction.

Pig: Financial matters will go well for the Pig in 1994, although he would do well to avoid any particularly speculative or risky ventures. With care, many Pigs can end the year in a much stronger financial position than at the start.

Career Prospects

Rat: A year of progress. All Rats would do well to make every effort to improve upon their present position. The Rat should go after any openings and opportunities that he sees. Persistence will bring its rewards!

Ox: An interesting year ahead! Although not all work-related matters may go as well as he would like, out of set-backs and disappointments, new and brighter opportunities will emerge for the Ox. By working hard and acting in a manner that he believes is right, he can and will make progress, particularly in the second half of the year.

Tiger: A rewarding and fulfilling time for the Tiger. He should promote his ideas and follow up any opportunities for advancement that he sees. With determination and hard work, many Tigers can make great strides in their career this year. It is also a favourable year for the Tiger to widen his experience, possibly by trying a different type of work.

Rabbit: A year of steady progress with many Rabbits gaining a new position or being given additional responsibilities. The knowledge, experience and skills that the Rabbit gains will serve him well in the future and all Rabbits would do well to try and further their skills over the year.

Dragon: A year of good and steady progress. The Dragon's talents, resourcefulness and quick thinking will be much appreciated by others and he will make pleasing advances in his career. However, 1994 is not a year when the Dragon can be over-ambitious in his activities or allow his rather impulsive nature to get the better of him.

Snake: A favourable year ahead. The Snake should promote his ideas as well as going after the several excellent opportunities that he will see over the year. He would also do well to remember that out of any changes that may take place, new opportunities and challenges will arise. It is these new opportunities that the Snake should seize. Many Snakes will be successful in gaining a new and better position over the year.

Horse: The Horse can make substantial progress in his career over the year. There will be several opportunities for him to better his position and he should pursue any openings that he sees. Anything that he can do to add to his skills will be to his future advantage.

Goat: A year of modest and steady progress. The Goat should try not to be over-ambitious in what he attempts over the year, but should concentrate on specific objectives. By working hard and adding to his skills, he will gain useful experience and this will do much to enhance his future prospects.

Monkey: Modest progress is indicated. The Monkey will need to work closely with others over the year and, while he does like to retain a certain amount of independence in his activities, he could find such an attitude working against him in 1994. Throughout the year, he should be open, willing and ready to co-operate with others, and remain positive.

Rooster: Much progress is possible. The Rooster should set about his work and objectives in his usual methodical way, pursue any openings that he sees and use any opportunity that he has to add to his skills and experience.

Dog: Career matters are most favourably aspected and the Dog should pursue any opportunities and openings that he sees. Great progress can be achieved and many Dogs will be successful in obtaining a new and better position.

Pig: A year of steady progress. The Pig should remain alert for opportunities to pursue and make every effort to expand his skills and experience. He should also give some thought to his future objectives. What he achieves in 1994 will help to lay the foundation for the substantial progress he will make over the next few years.

Relations with Others

Rat: Although usually adept at handling personal relationships, the Rat needs to tread carefully over the year if he wishes to preserve harmony around him. He needs to involve others in his activities and, despite the many demands on his time, he should regularly set some time aside to spend with his loved ones. To take the support of others for granted could cause problems!

Ox: Care is needed, particularly with work colleagues. Should any awkward situation arise, the Ox would do well to seek compromise rather than confrontation. His domestic life will be generally content and his social life will be busy. Many Oxen will form some new and important friendships over the year.

Tiger: A generally happy year. The Tiger's family and friends will give him much pleasure as well as being able to offer much valuable support and advice. Many Tigers will lead a busy social life over the year.

Rabbit: Domestically and socially, this will be a good and generally happy year. Many Rabbits will make some new and good friends over the year. Work colleagues may, however, prove difficult at times, but the Rabbit is very adept at handling relations with others and, with tact and diplomacy, any awkwardness can soon be overcome.

Dragon: Socially and domestically, a generally happy year. However, the Dragon does have a tendency to be rather forthright at times and if he is not careful, he could strain the normally good relations he enjoys with those around him. This is a year for tact and diplomacy. The Dragon would do well to involve others in his activities and take note of all that is going on around him. To adopt too independent an attitude could leave him lacking support when he needs it. A good year for making friends and for romance.

Snake: The Snake's relations with others will go well over the year, although he would do well to involve others in his activities and overcome his tendency to be secretive and independent!

Horse: Domestically and socially, this will be a good and happy year for the Horse. However, he should avoid the temptation of getting so thoroughly absorbed in his own concerns that he neglects the interests of

Goat: The Goat can look forward to some happy times with his family and friends. However, he would do well to seek their advice and support in times of uncertainty. Many Goats will make some new and important friends over the year.

Monkey: Both the Monkey's social and domestic life will give him much pleasure over the year. Those around him will be supportive and encouraging, but he does need to be more forthcoming in expressing his own views and feelings and not be so secretive.

Rooster: A good year both socially and domestically. Many Roosters will make some new and important friendships over the year. Romance is well aspected.

Dog: The Dog's home and social life are both likely to be most enjoyable, and for the single Dog, there will be many opportunities to build new and meaningful friendships.

Pig: A happy and sociable year ahead. Those around the Pig will be most supportive and if he feels under pressure or is in a dilemma, the Pig would do well to seek advice and help rather than deal with the matter single-handed. Many Pigs will establish some new and good friendships over the year.

Also available

YOUR PERSONAL HOROSCOPE 1994

Month-by-Month Forecasts for Every Sign

JOSEPH POLANSKY

Whatever your sign, *Your Personal Horoscope 1994* shows you how to make the most of your life in the coming year by taking full advantage of the planetary influences.

Sign by sign, the book includes:

- Yearly forecasts highlighting celestial trends for love and romance, home and the family, career and money
- Month-by-month forecasts pinpointing your best and worst days
- Penetrating character analyses – how each zodiac sign behaves with money, at work and in love
- Powerful insights into the lifestyles of each sign – their domestic and social life, health and relationships.

Understanding your own sign and the astrological influences for 1994 will help you bring out the best in yourself and the year to come.

Your Personal Horoscope 1994 is the next best thing to having your own personal astrologer!

YOUR PERSONAL HOROSCOPE 1994	1 85538 281 4	£6.99	☐
THE CHINESE ASTROLOGY WORKBOOK	0 85030 641 8	£7.99	☐
SUN SIGNS	1 85538 021 8	£4.99	☐
RISING SIGNS	0 85030 751 1	£4.99	☐
MOON SIGNS	0 85030 552 7	£5.99	☐
STAR QUALITY	1 85538 179 6	£4.99	☐
CHINESE ASTROLOGY	1 85538 232 6	£10.99	☐

All these books are available from your local bookseller or can be ordered direct from the publishers.

To order direct just tick the titles you want and fill in the form below:

Name: _____
Address: _____
_____
_____ Postcode: _____

Send to: Thorsons Mail Order, Dept 3, HarperCollins*Publishers*, Westerhill Road, Bishopbriggs, Glasgow G64 2QT.
Please enclose a cheque or postal order or your authority to debit your Visa/Access account —

Credit card no:_____
Expiry date: _____
Signature: _____

— up to the value of the cover price plus:
UK & BFPO: Add £1.00 for the first book and 25p for each additional book ordered.
Overseas orders including Eire: Please add £2.95 service charge. Books will be sent by surface mail but quotes for airmail despatches will be given on request.

24 HOUR TELEPHONE ORDERING SERVICE FOR ACCESS/VISA CARDHOLDERS — **TEL: 041 772 2281.**